The Buddha Mimansa

The Buddha and his relation to the religion of the Vedas

The Buddha Mimansa

The Buddha and his relation to the religion of the Vedas

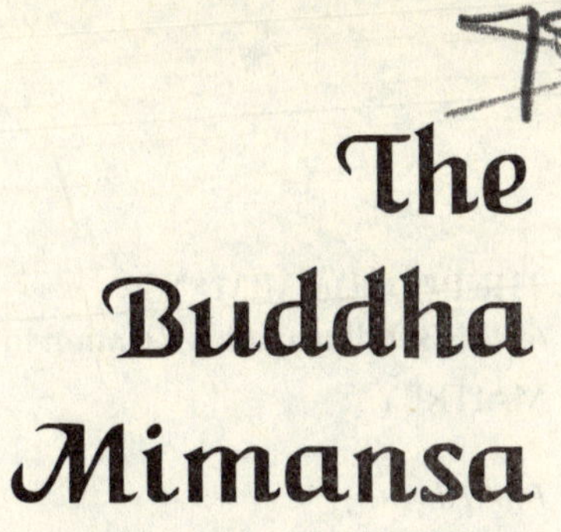

Being a collection of arguments with authoritative references and of notes with original texts, intended as materials for any future treatise on Buddhism

YOGIRAJA'S DISCIPLE MAITREYA

Edited by **His Holiness The Swami Maharaja Yogiraja**

PILGRIMS PUBLISHING
◆Varanasi◆

THE BUDDHA-MIMANSA
or the Buddha and his Relation to the Religion of the Vedas
MAITREYA

Published by:
PILGRIMS PUBLISHING

An imprint of:
PILGRIMS BOOK HOUSE
(Distributors in India)
B 27/98 A-8, Nawabganj Road
Durga Kund, Varanasi-221010, India
Tel: 91-542- 2314060, 2312456
E-mail: pilgrims@satyam.net.in
Website: www.pilgrimsbooks.com

PILGRIMS BOOK HOUSE (New Delhi)
9 Netaji Subhash Marg, 2nd Floor
Near Neeru Hotel, Daryaganj, New Delhi 110002
Tel: 91-11-23285081
E-mail: pilgrim@del2.vsnl.net.in

Distributed in Nepal by:
PILGRIMS BOOK HOUSE
P O Box 3872, Thamel, Kathmandu, Nepal
Tel: 977-1-4700942, Off: 977-1-4700919
Fax: 977-1-4700943
E-mail: pilgrims@wlink.com.np

First Published in 1925
Copyright © 2004, Pilgrims Publishing
All Rights Reserved

Cover design by Sasya

ISBN: 81-7769-089-2

Printed in India at Pilgrim Press Pvt. Ltd. Lalpur Varanasi

INTRODUCTION TO THE NEW EDITION

Religions worldwide have their ardent followers, who are in many instances ready to give up their lives for the precepts they believe to have no parallels. Still there are many who have a more enquiring nature and wish to understand those differences if any. The very concept of religion itself should lead the mind to consider and question certain aspects of what we are told. How far do these teachings really differ and if such differences are there how in fact do we actually decide upon their validity?

The Jews would have much to say about the teachings of say Christ or Mohammed and vice-versa though all claim to have their roots in the same basic beliefs. It is also true that many wars and acts of violence have taken place between them in the name of religion. In much the same way internecine clashes have taken place and still take place between the sects owing allegiance to these religious groups. It is this intolerance that has led to much grief and hardship in the world.

Much also has been said about the origins of Buddhism and the relationship that it has with the more ancient Vedic teachings of Sanatan Dharam, which form the basis of what know as present day Hinduism. There are many who will challenge this statement from the point of view that Hinduism is not a religion but only a reference to those living to the East of the River Indus. But for the sake of using terminology familiar to the vast majority let us continue to talk of Hinduism.

Maitreya has in this book discussed the so-called differences between the Buddhist teachings and those of the Vedas. He has quite convincingly pointed out that the Buddha born and brought up in Hindu society had not set out to set p a totally different philosophy but had actually taught and practiced within the bounds of the Vedic teachings. Throughout this book he has carefully pointed out that even the renowned Shankaracharya had like the Buddha deviated only nominally from the Vedic ways.

His main premise is, that the Buddha's only real deviation from the traditional ways of the Vedas was in those sections, which deal mainly with ritual and sacrifice. Saying it was something that the Buddha abhorred and wished to have removed from the daily practice of the Hindus. The author's treatise on relative religion provides an insight into the futility of the fundamentalist ideal of the continual conflict to establish the supremacy of something that is essentially similar. It also makes the reader ready to reconsider the preconceived and often much misunderstood ideals he may have formed about his own beliefs.

Christopher N Burchett
June 2003
Varanasi.

PREFACE

(By the Swami Maharaja Yogiraja of Buddha-Gaya)
(Translated)

At the instance of His Highness the Hon'ble Maharajadhiraja Sir Rameshwar Singh Bahadur of Darbhanga I offer the book to the public, hoping that it will be accorded a favourable reception by them. It is part of a comparative study of all Religions, made with a view to arrive at the Universal Religion. The whole range of Vedic and Buddhist literature, native as well as foreign, has been researched in preparing these pages, as will appear from a perusal of the book.

It gives me much pleasure to mention that the writer, Maitreya, belongs to the house of Gautama, which traces its Patriarchal descent from the Vedic Rishi Gotama, the founder of the Nyaya Philosophy or the first school of Logic in the world. A scion of the same house was Gautama Buddha, the founder of Buddhism and the subject of the present treatise.

I have further pleasure in mentioning that our worthy and esteemed District Magistrate, W. B. Brett, Esq., I.C.S., has taken the trouble of going through the pages, and I quote his appreciation below.

—— o ——

I have read the book " The Buddha and his Relation to the Religion of the Vedas " with much interest.

(Sd.) W. B. BRETT.

Extract from a letter received from
His Excellency the Right Honourable Rufus Daniel Isaacs,
EARL OF READING, P.C., G.C.B., G.M S.I., G M I.E., G.C.V.O.,
Viceroy and Governor-General of India.

———

D. O. No. 1016-C.

PRIVATE SECRETARY'S
OFFICE :

VICEROY'S CAMP,
INDIA.

To

YOGIRAJA'S DISCIPLE MAITREYA.

DEAR SIR,

I am desired to acknowledge with thanks the receipt of a copy of " The Buddha Mimansa, " which has been placed before His Excellency the Viceroy. *His Excellency was much interested to read it.*

Yours truly,
C. P. HANCOCK.

PREAMBLE.

Whereas there has been a long-standing difference between Hindus and Buddhists on account of which the Swami Maharaja Yogiraja of Buddha-Gaya has been repeatedly asked by Princes and the Public of India to do something in the way of making up the difference, it is therefore expedient that the following pages which have been prepared at the Yogiraja's behest and under his auspices be laid before the Representatives of the two Religions with a view to establish harmony and **peaceful co-operation** between contending parties, a more laudable task than which there cannot be.

Peoples of the world are agreed that strifes about minor points of religion are worse than useless, the main point of all the various systems of religion being one and the same. The Problem of the Infinite and the Riddle of the Universe are not for man to solve so long as his mind is confined and limited by his body. But Science and Philosophy, though still in their infancy, have given ample proofs of the strength of the unconquerable mind and the weakness of matter as compared with it. Man's nearest concern is, therefore, how to step into the next higher stage of evolution (which, according to Science, is yet to come ; or which, according to Revelation, is already in existence), in which the body is brought under sway of mind. It is this concern for the uplift of the race that takes the form of the various systems of religion, which all begin with some authenticated communication of man with the higher beings (devas, seraphs, malekhs, fravashis, angels, gods, immortals).

The book consists of two parts. The first part terminates on p. 76. The second part contains several texts which appeared before in a pamphlet named " Buddha-Gaya Māhātmya : Texts about Buddha and Buddha-Gaya, or Buddha-Gaya a Hindu Shrine," prepared by the Yogiraja himself and spoken of as a most valuable compilation for all Hindus by the late Hon'ble Justice Dr. Sir Gurudas Banerji, Kt., M.A., LL.D., PhD., of the High Court of Judicature at Fort William in Bengal. It was originally printed for free distribution among the Spiritual Heads, Foreign Potentates, Indian Ruling Chiefs, and Representative Scholars.

It is obvious that all well-founded criticisms of these pages will be helpful to the writer who has tried his best to look at the subject-matter from the stand-point of truth. Communications may be sent to the writer at the Maharajadhiraja of Darbhanga's House, Chowringhee, Calcutta.

MAITREYA.
Disciple of the Yogiraja of Buddha-Gaya.

CONTENTS

First Part.

Second Part.

OBSERVATIONS.

THE words " See **N** " in the foot-notes mean that elaborations and original texts are to be found in the Notes at the end of the book.

Figures separated by hyphens indicate the sub-divisions of the book referred to. For example, Rig Veda 1-1-2, means Rig Veda, first Mandala, first Sukta, second Mantra. Similarly in all other cases.

THE BUDDHA=MIMANSA.

THE OBEISANCE.

Lord of Infinite Majesty, more merciful than the creator ; surpassing the sun in the dispelling of darkness ; excelling the moon in the allaying of heat ; such is the peerless Buddha to whom obeisance is being done here.[1]

INTRODUCTION.

The Sanatana Dharma, or Religion of the Vedas.

In the history of religions the broad features of the Sanātana Dharma or the World-old Religion of the Vedas have been traced. The World-old Religion concerns itself neither with matter nor with mind. It knows of a third thing, namely, spirit (or soul), of which both matter and mind are manifestations[2] ; and it directs all its activities to

Vedic Religion. Elements of the Creed : I. Spirit.

---

[1] The Buddha-Charita of Aswaghosa I—I (See **N**).

[2] This is the theme of all the Upanishads and of the teachings of Plato in ancient and Hegel in modern times. See Sully's "Human Mind" : Vol. II. Appendix, p. 369, and Green's "Prolegomena to Ethics," Art. 33. (See **N**).

the perfect comprehension of this thing only.[1] It holds that by such perfect comprehension,—that by it alone and by no other means,—all the mysteries of matter and mind are also cleared up.[2] It holds the spirit to be something powerful,—creative,—and this power of the spirit it calls the will.[3] It

2. Power. believes in the strength of the unconquerable will and the weakness of matter and mind as compared with it[4]; in the gradual triumph of the will over matter and mind, securing the final liberation of the pure spirit from all connections with the vile body

---

[1] Brihadaranyaka Upanishad 4-5-6 ; Mundaka Upanishad 2-2-5. (See **N**).

[2] Chhandogya Upanishad 6-1-3 ; Brihadaranyaka Upanishad 4-5-6. Cf. the Bible : Job xxxii, 8 ; Proverbs xx, 27 ; Ecclesiastes xii, 7 ; John iv, 24 ; I Corinthians xiv, 2. (See **N**).

[3] Schopenhauer has bequeathed this term to the new metaphysics of Europe. (Weber : " History of Philosophy," p. 556. foot-note). The will is the *Sakti* or *Māyā* of the Vedas and Tantras, It is the Druj of the Avesta. (Smith's " Cyclopædia of Names," under the word ' Ahura Mazda'). (See **N**).

[4] Cf. Dr. Charles Mackay's " Memoirs of Extraordinary Popular Delusions," 2nd Ed.,—the chapter on the Magnetisers (conclusion). This magnetic power of the will over matter and mind affords an illustration of the words of the inspired Psalmist that we are " fearfully and wonderfully made." (Bible : Psalms cxxxix, 14).

and the impure mind ;—which liberation it calls the
salvation (Videhamukti ; Nirvāna)[1]. It
3. The Devas. knows of the existence of beings superior
to man in the scale of evolution (the devas, gods,
spirits, angels),[2] in whom the will-power has so far
triumphed as to bring the body (and matter) under the
sway of the mind, thus ensuring a partial liberation to

---

[1] This is the theme of the Vedanta Philosophy of Sankarāchārya. The term " Nirvāna " was used in the Upanishads and
the Yogavāsistha long before the coming of Buddha. It is wrongly
supposed to be a term of Buddhistic origin. See the term
" Brahma-nirvana " in the Bhagavad-Gita (2-72).

Dr. Savory in the introduction to the " Book of Health "
takes up the subject from a scientific point of view and supports
the saying of St. Paul that the body is a humiliation to the soul
and that it shall be changed. (" Book of Health," edited by
Malcolm Morris, Introductory chapter).

[2] The Taittiriya Upanishad : 2-8. Cf. Brihadaranyaka
Upanishad : 4-3-33. Also Bible : Daniel, vii, 10 ff. (See **N**).
The hosts of celestial beings are called the " upper family "
(Ephesians iii, 15) and with reference to them God is called the
Lord of Hosts (Zachariah viii). The Koran also says that God
employs the Angels as envoys, guardians, guides, and revealers to
mankind (Koran ; Surah : 13-12 ; 16-2 ; 35-1 ; 42-51). Muhammad
himself declared that the Koran was delivered to him, with God's
order to preach it, by the Angel Gabriel (Koran ; Surah : 2-91 ;
42-52 ; 53-1). (See **N**). And so, in spite of Muhammad's prohibition, there are many spirit-worshippers among his followers, who
ignite the sacred lamp at the graves of their saints. [" The devas,
or gods, of the different heavens are of the same class with angels
and saints."—See Prinsep : " Tibet, Tartary and Mongolia,"
p. 140]. The Parsi and Chinese Religions not only believe in
spirits but are based upon fire-worship. [On the worship of the
Sacred Fire among the Chinese, and on Fire-worship as Ancestor-
worship, see Frazer's " Golden Bough," Vol. X, p. 136 ff., and
Vol. II, p. 221].

(4)

the spirit (Jivanmukti). It lays down that man's nearest task is to elevate himself to the level of the Devas, and prescribes various methods for the fulfilment of that task. Thus the Religion of the Vedas,[1] like the Religion of the Bible,[2] prescribes the worship of the Sacred Fire,[3] holding that Fire is the only medium of communication with the celestial hosts who are beings with fiery bodies (Seraphs, lit. burning beings)[4] ; and who therefore make their appearance in fire only, which is

4. Fire-Worship.

---

[1] All the Vedas open with a glowing tribute to the Sacred Fire as its cynosure,—" the polar star to sailors on life's pathless seas." (Mahābhārata, Banaparva 200-13). Cf. "The Vedas have been revealed for the due worship by man of the Devas." (Mahābhārata : Sāntiparva Mokshadharma 327-50). (See **N**).

[2] The Religion of the Bible, together with its Temple, had its origin in the Hallowed Fire of Moses. See Exodus iii, 2 ; xix, 18 ; Deuteronomy v, 25-26 ; Leviticus ix, 23-24 ; vi, 12-13 ; II Chronicles vii, 1 ; I Kings xviii, 38 ; Numbers iv, 13 ; Isaiah vi, 4-5 ; Ezekiel i, 4 ; Revelation i, 13-15 ; II Thessalonians i, 8 ; Acts ii, 3 ; Daniel vii, 10 ; Exodus xiii, 21. (See **N**).

[3] Other methods are also prescribed (whether conjoined to fire-worship or not), e.g. the Yoga and the Tantra, both of which are for elevating man to the level of the Devas.

[4] Bible : Isaiah, Ch. 6 ; Mahābhārata, Banaparva 261-13 ; Aniruddha on the Sankhya Philosophy : 5-112. Rig Veda 9-113-4. (See **N**).

their proper element.[1] To indicate their creed the votaries of the Sanātana Dharma generally wear a tuft of hair on their heads called the Shikhā (which word literally means the burning flame), build their temples in the shape of a flame (bulging out at the base and tapering up to a point)[2] ; and worship the cow because her butter is ordained as the proper thing to be poured into the fire to make it

5. The cow.

---

[1] Rig Veda 1-1-2 ; 1-12-1 ; 1-22-10. (See **N**). The fire which is the proper element of the Devas in which they choose to make themselves visible to man is that which is first generated by the process of friction known as *Pramathana* in the Vedas, from which comes the Greek mythology of Prometheus stealing fire from heaven. (See Kaegi : " Rig Veda," p. 132 of the English Translation. Also Kuhn and Schmidt). Shakespeare alludes to it as having a life-giving power,—as a restorer of the departed spirit to the dead body :—" That Promethean heat that can thy light relume." (Othello 5-2-12).

[2] There are three types of temples, each indicating by its outward shape the kind of worship which is ordained within it. The round-topped temples (domes, mosques) are for worship of the male element, the *Lingam* or Phallus ; the triangular-faced temples (cones or pyramids) are for worship of the female element, the *Yoni* ; and the flame-shaped temples are for the worship of the Sacred Fire. (Cf. Jennings : " Nature Worship," Phallicism, p. 55-56). Within each of these Fire-temples there was a triangle-shaped spot at the base called the " Yoni " (or place of origin) in the Vedas, in which Ghrita (or melted butter) was kept burning. (Rig Veda 1-140-1 ; 3-5-7). (See **N**). Cf. also Goldstucker : " Literary Remains," Vol. I, p. 25, and Stevenson's Introduction to Sama Veda). Right above the burning Ghrita was suspended a jar (full of that Ghrita), called the Kumbha (Atharva Veda 3-12-8), (See **N**), which fed the fire by letting fall continuous drops of Ghrita on it (" Ghritasya dhārā " :—Rig Veda, 4-58—5 to 8). (See **N**). In former times, periodical gatherings of these *Kumbhas*

(the fire) sacred to the Devas : for, not all fire but that which burns upon some fatty substance[1] is held to be sacred to the Devas.   Further, the Sanātana-Dharmins ignite the fire to purify a birth, to bear witness to a marriage, and, finally, to consume the dead.   They

6. Sacredness of marriage and chastity.

further hold that human marriages are sacred and elevate the pair to the heaven of the Devas if chastity has been faithfully preserved by both the parties ; and hence is the origin of Sakti-pujā or Female-worship among them.

---

taking place at *Prayagas,* or centres of fire-worship, were popularly known as the Kumbha-melas. Subsequently, when Ghrita had become too dear through the exportation and slaughter of cows by foreigners (Rig Veda 10-108) (See **N**), a stone, which originally had nothing to do with the Phallus with which it has been hopelessly confounded,—was substituted for the Fire, as the *Lingam* or a symbol for it, and a jar of dropping water for the Ghrita-Kumbha. (Cf. Mahabharata : Banaparva 228-5 ; 229-27). (See **N**). The Kumbha-mela now survives in name only.

[1] The fat of the ram in the Bible (Leviticus vi, 12 ; ix, 19). The Rig Veda eschews such fats and prefers cow's butter as having a superior efficacy. In the Bible, however, there is a prophecy of the protection of the cow and the profuse use of her butter in the Renaissance to come with the Messiah. (See Isaiah vii, 21-22). (See **N**).

CHAPTER I.

Buddha himself a follower of the Religion of the Hindus.

Gautama Buddha was a product of the World-old Religion of the Vedas (the Sanatana Dharma or Hinduism proper), and the religion which he is supposed to have given to the world was not any new religion as it is sometimes wrongly maintained to be, but only a reformation of the extravagances and corruptions which had crept into the existing system of the World-old Religion at that time.[1] He came from the Kshatriya or warrior tribe of India, and his name Sākya Singha attests to it ; the word Singha being always added to the proper names of the Kshatriyas.[2] He was a Nepali by birth, being born at Kapila-vāstu or the abode

Buddha a Nepali Kshatriya by birth : born in a stronghold of Hinduism.

---

[1] See the extracts from authorities, at the end of the present work. Cf. " In its origin at least, Buddhism was more of a social than of a religious reformation. It was an attack upon that web of priestcraft which Brahmanism had woven round the Society." (Smith : " Mohammed and Mohammedanism," p. 4). Cf. Max Muller : " Chips from a German Workshop," Vol. I, p. 220 ; Spence Hardy : " Legends and Theories of the Buddhists," Intro., p. 13-20 ; Beal : " Buddhist Pilgrims," Intro., p. 49, ff. Cf. Powell : " Buddha, the Reformer of Brahmism " (Utica, U.S.A.) ; also cf. Clarke : " Buddhism, or The Protestantism of the East " (Atlantic Monthly, Boston, Vol. XXIII, p. 713 ff.).

[2] Cunningham, with his usual sagacity, perceived the real name of Buddha when he prepared the inscription within the Great Temple of Buddha-Gaya wherein occurs the following :—" Where Prince Sakya Singha became Buddha." (See **N**). Cf. Hunter's

of the Rishi Kapila of old. His father,—a Kshatriya (Singha) whose real name is apparently lost, was a Hindu of the orthodox type, noted for the purity of his food whence he received the appelation of *Suddhodana,* or the pure vegetarian.[1] The Buddha was thus born[2] and brought up in the cradle of the purest form of Hinduism and was himself a follower of the World-old

A vegetarian from birth.

" Gaya and Shahabad," p. 53 ; Sherring's " Benares," p. 5 (Sakya Muni). During the period between the renunciation of home and the attainment of Buddhahood, Buddha was known by the name of Sakya Muni :—and it is a fact that the word Muni, whenever applied to a person, is applied to his native name. Marco Polo who visited India in 1250 A. D., found the Buddha generally known as the Sakya Muni (Sagamoni).—Book iii, Ch. 15. (Cordier's Ed., Vol. II, p. 316). [Cf. Sandor Csoma Korosi : " Notices on the life of Shakya, extracted from the Tibetan authorities." (Asiatic Researches, Calcutta, 1836, Vol. XX, p. 285-317)].

[1] It might be observed here that no such another name of this kind is to be found in the history of the contemporary times, from which it is not unreasonable to infer that it was not a name but an appellation derived from some peculiar tiait in the character of that person to whom it was applied. Nepal has always been a land of professed meat-eaters, and any one abjuring meat entirely would naturally receive a distinctive appellation on that account.

[2] Cf. Hemadri, Bratakhanda, Ch. 15 :—" In this way by his observances of fast, by Suddhodana (pure food), was brought into birth the Supreme Spirit as Buddha " (*as his son :*—in Bhavisya Puran). (See **N**).

(9)

Religion of the Vedas.   One of the appellations given to

A   fire-wor-shipper. him is *Arkabandhu*, which means " Friend of the Sun."[1]   Evidently this means that he was pre-eminent for his regular devotions to the sun, which is only another form of fire-worship.[2]   Indeed, there are many indications of fire-worship to be found in the Religion of the Buddha and the different schools of his followers.[3]   The Vedic rites of the Sacred Fire (*Yajna*) required the worshipper to cover his head with a turban (the " *Usnisa* " or *Sirastrāna*).   The Rishis wore this turban and Buddha also

---

[1] See the Sanskrit Lexicons :—Amarakosha 1-1-1-10 ; Abhidhana-Chintamani of Hemachandra 2-149 ff ; Vaijayanti-kosha of Yadavaprakash : 1-1-35 (Oppert).   (See **N**).

[2] Fire-worshippers worship the Sun also, which is the Central Fire of the Universe.   " The relation of fire to the sun is unmistakable.   The Japanese call fire and sun by the same name, *hi*." (Aston : " Shinto," p. 159).   The name Mithraism or Sun-worship (the sun being called *Mithra* in the Avesta, and *Mitra* in the Vedas) is applied to the Fire-worship of the Parsis.   Cf. also Rig Veda 3-5-4 ; 10-45-1. (See **N**).

[3] Buddha recommended the worship of the Sacred Fire and himself practised it (see Arya Manjusri Mulakalpa, Ch. xiii) ; and he always chose to sit beneath the tree (the *Aswattha*) whose wood was specially consecrated to purposes of the Sacred Fire (Rhys Davids : " Buddhist India," p. 231).   Cf. Hargrave Jennings : " The Results of the Mysterious Buddhism," (Ch. 23 and elsewhere).   (See **N**).

was never without it.[1] His place of worship is called the *Chaitya*, which word originally means the place of the Sacred Fire.[2] His temple, though having characteristics peculiar to itself, is unmistakably of the flame-type, and his followers still bear testimony to this fact of their original fire-worship by wearing the tuft of hair called " *Shikhā* " (literally, the flame) on their heads ; by protecting and venerating the cow ; and by profusely using the Ghrita or melted butter for illuminations and other acts of devotion.[3] Even in

---

[1] The Vedas enjoined the *Usnisha* (or head-dress) for all fire-worshippers (Atharva Veda 15-2-1 ; Aitareya Brahmana 6-1 ; Aswalayana Srauta Sutra 5-12 ; Katyayana Srauta Sutra 22-4-10.) [See Waddell: "Buddha's Diadem or 'Usnisa'"; a study of Buddhist origins (Berlin) ; and cf. the title of the book : "Ushnisha-vijaya-dharani" (Oxford)]. (See **N**).

[2] [Cf. Narayan Aiyangar : Chaityas. (Indian Antiquary, Bombay, 1882 ; Vol. II)]. The word *chaitya* is derived from the word *chitya*, which means fire (Panini 3-1-132). Hence *chaitya* means the " place of *Yajna* or sacred fire ." (See Shabdakalpa-druma under both the words). (See **N**).

[3] [Cf. the " Pradipa-dāniya Sutra " of the Buddhists, dealing with the rites of offering lights of burning Ghrita]. Even now Buddhist pilgrims may be seen at Buddha-Gaya and other places of their worship offering large quantities of Ghrita to be burnt before the image of the Buddha. In the Great Temple of Buddha-Gaya, on the floor towards which the eyes of the Buddha-image seem to be directed, is a large circular mark wherein was originally a pit for burning Ghrita, which was afterwards converted into a place for the *Lingam*, as was done in all the fire-temples of India when Ghrita became dear.

the distant Pamirs, there is still the " flame in the butter " in front of the images of Buddha.[1]

Like all fire-worshippers, Buddha declared the existence of Devas or heavenly beings, both of the higher and the lower kinds, and of several unseen Lokas (world-systems or celestial spheres) for their abode.[2] He spoke of Indra (the Devarāja), of Brahmā (the Sahampati or Sabhāpati), of Kuvera (the Yaksharaja) and of Māra (the Kāmadeva),—all Devas of the Hindu Pantheon,—as paying occasional visits to him. And his followers, consequently, have mixed up his system with the idolatrous Tantras, which are nothing but the worship of the Devas through the sacred fire.[3]

A believer in the Devas.

---

[1] Lord Dunmore : " The Pamirs," Vol. I, p. 145.

[2] Rhys Davids : " The Buddhist Suttas," p. 88, p. 154. (See **N**).

[3] (See **N**). Dr. Enriquez in his " Images in Buddhism " speaks of idolatry in Buddhism as a surprising fact. Cf. Knebel : " The Vāhanas of the Brahmanical and Buddhistic Pantheon." (Tijdschrift voor Indische Kunde, Batavia, deel 47, p. 227-340).

(12)

And as he was a Hindu,[1] Buddha respected the caste-system of the Sanātana Dharma.

A respecter of the caste. There are texts to prove it and they are of special significance as being found in professedly Buddhist Scriptural works. " The Bodhisattwa or Buddha-elect regards caste distinctions. He never takes birth in the lower castes ; (therefore) he takes birth only in one of the two higher castes, namely, the caste of Brahmana or (the caste) of Kshatriya."[2] " Having made such a noble sacrifice, the meritorious man is to be born a Bodhisattwa or Buddha-elect in some illustrious family of the Kshatriya tribe or (in some illustrious family) of the Brahmana tribe."[3]

---

[1] **On Buddha's *being a Hindu*,** cf. Waddell : " Buddha's Secret, from a Sixth Century Commentary." (Journal of the Royal Asiatic Society, London, 1894, p. 372).

[2] Lalita Vistara, Ch. 3, line 146 ff. (Lefmann's edition). (See **N**). " Several of the Pre-historic Buddhas (Purva Buddhas) were Brahmans."—Sherring's " Benares," p. 153. The Buddhavansa represents the majority of previous Buddhas as Brahmans and only a few as Kshatriyas. The observance of caste rules by Brahmans was recommended by Buddha, and he generally accepted Brahmans as his own disciples. (See Copleston : " Buddhism Past and Present," Ch. 16). Buddha did not denounce the caste theory but exploded the doctrine that salvation is not open to all castes. [Cf. Chalmers : " The Madhura Sutra" (Journal of the Royal Asiatic Society, 1894, p. 348)].

[3] Satasāhasrikā Prajnāpāramitā (See **N**).

" He is never born in the lower castes : this is a distinctive mark of the Bodhisattwa." " The Bodhisattwa is born of a high caste, the caste of Kshatriya or the caste of Brahmana ; he is born in the very lineage to which belonged the preceding Bodhisattwas."[1]

And as he observed the caste-system so he observed the regulations of food enjoined by the World-old Religion. He even went beyond it in prohibiting all dainty articles of diet, e.g., milk and its products, for the *Sramanas* (Sannyāsins, ascetics).[2] Doubtless he permitted the *Sramanas* to take the unprohibited foods from all givers irrespective of their castes, just as he used to do himself ; and in this respect Sankarāchārya and his followers (the Sannyāsins of India), who are regarded as the spiritual heads of the Hindu Religion, are also

An observer of food-regulations.

---

[1] Satasāhasrikā-Prajnāpāramitā, Ch. 10, p. 1460, and p. 1471 (Asiatic Society's edition). (See **N**).

[2] An enumeration of the permitted and of the prohibited foods is to be found in the Bhikshu Prātimoksha Sutra. (Cf. Oldenberg : " Vinaya Texts," Vol. I, p. 40). It may be observed here that the term *Sramana* adopted by Buddha for himself and his followers was not a word of his invention but may be found in the Rāmāyana of the Hindus in the sense of an ordinary Sannyāsin (or ascetic).—See the Rāmāyana of Valmiki, Balakanda xiv—12. (See **N**).

much on the same level. It may be noted here that Buddha followed the World-old Religion **An ordainer of cremation.** in the matter of consigning the remains of the dead to the fire, while Sankarā-chārya departed from it and ordained the alien custom of burying the dead for his followers.

The story of Buddha's death at Kusinārā from the effects of ingesting " dried boar's flesh " **Story of Buddha's death.** while at Pāva, is a fallacy supported by a falsehood. True, the Buddhist Scriptures say that Buddha died by eating of " *suska sukara-mārdava* "; and the term *suska* means " dried." But the other term, *sukara-mardava*, which literally means " soft as the boar's flesh," is the name of the mushroom plant.[1] It is some modern translator who has promulgated this false story of Buddha's death by mistranslating the word *sukara-mārdava* into " boar's flesh."

Dried boar's flesh is a thing unknown,—boar's flesh being too fatty an article to be brought to the dried state without becoming putrid and

---

[1] Cf. Khunnilal Sastri of Bareilly in his able article on " Buddha as a Believer." See Neumann : " Die Raden Gotama Buddho's " ; cf. Nariman : " Tiel's Religion of the Iranian People," preface, p. 6. Also Silachara's Catechism. (Neumann takes *sukara-mārdava* as equal to the Sanskrit word *sukra-mārdava*).

unwholesome. Especially in Pāva,—a land teeming with living boars all the year round in all ages,—dried boar's flesh can have no reason for existence. Buddha, born and bred in the house of Suddhodana (who derived his appellation from the purity of his food), and himself exhorting the whole world to desist from the slaughter of animals, would have been the last person to take dried boar 's flesh, which must be disgusting even to the palate of the professed meat-eater. Chanda, who offered him the last meal of his life, was a Hindu gold-smith[1] by caste to whom boar was untouchable by the immemorial usages of the land. The Muhammadans, to whom boar's flesh is prohibited as " hārām " by their religion itself, are very bitter in their invectives and abuses upon all eaters of that article. Yet it is a strange fact that nowhere in the vast Muhammadan literature of sectarian polemics have abuses been poured forth upon Buddha for having been an eater of the detestable " hārām." On the contrary, such authoritative and classical Muhammadan works as the Shahristani speak reverentially of him. The allegation that Buddha died by eating of dried

---

[1] Oldenberg: " Buddha," p. 200. Rhys Davids speaks of him as a copper-smith. See " Buddhist Suttas," p. 73.

boar's flesh is, therefore, unsupported by facts. The term " dried " and the season of Buddha's death are of great significance in determining this point. *Applied to boar's flesh it has no meaning : applied to mushroom it explains and clears up the whole thing.* The poorer classes of the people of Pāva and Kusinārā, where Buddha died, may still be found eating mushroom fresh in the rainy season, which is its proper season, and preserving it in the dried state to serve when its season is over. This article of diet is spoken of in bad terms by medical authorities ; it is always difficult of digestion, and some varieties of it are poisonous and often cause death with symptoms of dysentery.[1] Buddha died of dysentery, and died in the spring season.[2] Evidently, then, if mushroom was taken by him before his death, it must have been taken in the dried state at that season of the year. And this offers a good explanation of the expression " *suska sukara-mārdava* " in the story of Buddha's death. The imputation of meat-eating was falsely made to his name by Devadatta, his worst enemy,

---

[1] Bhāvaprakāsa (First Portion) : Sākavarga 105-107. As to their nutritive value and as to some varieties of them being poisonous, see Lorand : Health and Longevity through Rational Diet, pp. 241—246.—" Even the edible varieties of them may, at times, have a poisonous action as they become very rapidly decomposed when kept for any length of time." " A good stomach and intestine are required for their digestion." (Lorand).

[2] Rhys Davids : " The Buddhist Suttas ", p. 72.

whom he used always to forgive with a god-like forgiveness.[1] Such a thing should not be mentioned at all except that it is referred to by way of vindicating the unimpeachable conduct of this personality who was above the possibility of all inconsistencies. The Buddhist priests of the higher class still follow the example of their revered teacher and abstain from meat rigidly.[2]

Both in morals and in philosophy Buddha followed **A follower of the Vedic Rishis :—** in the footsteps of the Vedic Rishis. His veneration for them is evinced by his frequent mention of the sayings of the Rishis of the Vedas as his authority, whom he used to include in the term Purva-Buddhas or the Buddhas of old[3]; and by his expressly saying that he chose Benares as

---

[1] When his followers would combine to punish any of his calumniators, Buddha would make them desist from taking such a course and would only instruct them to plead his innocence (Cf. the Digha Nikāya, Brahma-jāla Sutra, § 5 ff).

[2] Cf. "Binning's Travels," Vol. I, p. 19. Cf. also Hopkins : "The Buddhist rule against eating meat" (Journal of American Oriental Society, New Haven, 1907, Vol. XXVII, p. 457 & seq.).

[3] Cf.—La Vallée Poussin : "On the authority (prāmānya) of the Buddhist Āgamas" (Journal of the Royal Asiatic Society, London, 1902, p. 374).—George Buehler : "Buddha's quotation of a Gāthā by Sanatkumara" (Journal of the Royal Asiatic Society, London, 1897, p. 585 ff.).—Watanabe : "The story of Kalmāsa-pāda. A Study in the Mahabharata and the Jātaka." (Journal of the Pali Text Society, London, 1909, p. 236-310).—Hardy : "The story of the merchant Ghosaka, with reference to other Indian parallels" (Journal of the Royal Asiatic Society, London, 1898, p. 787 ff).

the place where to begin his mission of reformation
because it was the old and venerable place of the
Rishis of old.[1]   The Vinaya Sutras or
—in morals ;
moral codes of the Buddhist canon are
apparently a recapitulation of the Grihya Sutras of the
Hindu Scriptures.[2]   His prohibition of the slaughter of
living animals, and of killing in general, was based on
the authority of well-known Vedic Texts which he

---

[1] Lalita Vistara, Ch. 25 (towards the end of the Chapter).
(See **N**).

[2] Cf. Fuehrer : " Manusāra-dhamma-sattham, the Buddhist
law book compared with the Brahmanical Mānava-dharma-sāstram
or Manu Samhita " (Journal of the Royal Asiatic Society, Bombay,
1882, Vol. XV, p. 333 ff) ;—Edmund Hardy on Pali canon as
coming from the Grihya Sutras of the Vedas : " Der Grhya-Ritus
pratyavarohana im Pali-Kanon " (Deutsche Morgenlandische
Gesellschaft. Zeitschrift. Leipzig, Band 52, p. 149-151) ;—Franke:
" Die Gathas des Vinayapitaka und ihre Parallelen " (Vienna,
1910). [For Brahmanic precedent in Buddhism, see Max Muller :
" Dhammapada," p. 28. On the Relation of Buddhist Sacred
Books to Satapatha Brahmana, see Kern : " Saddharma-Punda-
rika," p. **xvi** ff ; and to Mahabharata and Manu-Smriti, see Buhler :
" The Laws of Manu," p. **xci**, note].

quoted verbatim.[1] His doctrine of universal love is based upon the principle of conquering hatred by non-hate, which is thoroughly Vedic in its origin.[2] And he upheld the Vedic doctrine of the sacredness of marriage and hated unchastity with a genuine hatred.[3]

Like the Rishis he believed in the soul and its re-birth in the life to come, and in the law of retribution (*Karma*) which visits evil-doing with evil and good-doing with good.[4]

—in philosophy;

---

[1] Vedic Text : " Don't slay any living being " (quoted by Sridhara Swamin in Bhagavad-Gita 18-3). It is worth noting that the dictum *Ahinsā paramodharma* (giving up of slaughter is the height of religion) was not first pronounced by Buddha, as is wrongly supposed by many, but occurs in the Mahabharata more than once. (See **N**).

[2] The Vedas say : " One should bridge over the otherwise unbridgable stream of hatred by non-hate " (The Sama Veda, Chhanda Archika, Ch. 6, pt. 1, mantra 9). Buddha puts it thus : " Let one overcome hatred by love. Hatred does not cease by hating at any time ; hatred ceases by not hating : this is its nature." (Dhammapada 17-3 ; Dhammapada 1-5). (See **N**).

[3] See Rhys Davids : " Buddhist Suttas," p. 91. (See **N**).

[4] " Being a Hindu he (the Buddha) adopted the then, as now, current Hindu notion of metempsychosis or palingenesis,—from death to re-birth and fresh deaths to fresh re-births."—Waddell : "Buddha's Secret from a Sixth Century Commentary" (Journal of the Royal Asiatic Society, London, 1894, p. 372). Cf.—Gough : " The Philosophy of the Upanishads," p. 186.—Krishnamacharyya : " Buddhism ; its fundamental beliefs." (Brahmavadin, 1911). [Ananda Maitriya holds a different view in his Transmigration]. (See **N**).

Like them he believed in the Yoga philosophy[1]; practised it himself,[2] became the prince of Yogins,[3] and taught it to others as well.[4] He even acquired the highest power of the Yogin, the power to recollect the series of previous births (Jātismaratwa).[5] His Metaphysics, too, is no other than that of the Vedic

---

[1] Buddhacharita of Aswaghosha : Ch. 12, ver. 103 (Oxford Ed.). (See **N**). The original texts show that the Buddha was a firm believer in the Yoga, and did not try its methods by way of experiment only. [Cf. Hermann Jacobi : " On the relation of the Buddhistic philosophy to Sankhya-Yoga and the signification of the Nidānas " (Zeitschrift der Deutschen Morgenlandischen Gesellschaft, Band 52, pp. 1—15). Cf. Monier Williams : " Mystical Buddhism in connection with the Yoga Philosophy of the Hindus " (Victoria Institute, Annual Report, 1888, London). Also cf. Senart : " Bouddhisme et Yoga " (Review of the History of Religions, Paris, Vol. XLII)].

[2] Cf. the Jātaka-sasthi Pujāprakaranam, verse 2 ; and Vayu Purana 18—28. (See **N**).

[3] Cf. Sankarāchārya's Hymn to Buddha in his Dasavatara stotra. (See **N**).

[4] Hence grew up the sect of Yogāchāras in Buddhism.

[5] This is the theme of all the Jātaka Tales of Buddhism. Cf. the saying of Krishna in the Bhagavad-Gita, 4—5. (See **N**).

[It is not generally known that Æsop's Fables had their origin in the Jātakas, and the Arabian Nights' Entertainment in the Brihat-katha of Budha Swamin.—See Fytche, " Burma Past and Present," Vol. II, p. 144].

Rishis.[1] One of his accepted names is Advaya-vādin,[2] which means a true follower of the Upanishads,—one who maintains the doctrine of the real existence of the one thing only. This one thing or the Thing-in-itself in his philosophy is the same as the Infinitude of Consciousness (or Pure Spirit) arrived at by the Aryans and set forth in the World-old Religion of the Vedas as the " Jnānam-anantam " (or Brahma)[3] ; and, to indicate its Aryan origin, Buddha calls it by the name of "Ārya Prajnā-pāramitā," and applies to it epithets of Vedic coinage, as *amita* (infinite), *nirvikalpa* (absolute), etc.[4] This is the Vedic *Brahmavāda* in his philosophy ; and there is also the corresponding *Māyāvāda* in it under the name of *Sunyavāda*. By *Sunyatā* or nothingness, more correctly, emptiness or

---

[1] Cf. La Vallée Poussin : " Mahāyāna Buddhism " (Journal of the Royal Asiatic Society, London, 1908, p. 889) ; Oldenberg : " Die Religion des Veda und der Buddhismus " (Deutsche Rundschau, Berlin, 1895, Vol. LXXXV).

[2] The Lexicons, Amarakosha 1-1-1-9 ; and Vaijayanti-kosha 1-1-34. (See **N**).

[3] Taittiriya Upanishad 2-1. (See **N**).

[4] The Abhidharmapitaka (Introductory Hymn to the Prajnā-pāramitā Astasahasrika). Cf. " As a Religion, Buddhism is often alleged to be atheistic. But Buddha, as is well-known, nowhere expressly denies an Infinite First Cause or an unconditioned Being beyond the finite."—Waddell : " Buddha's Secret from a Sixth Century Commentary " (Journal of the Royal Asiatic Society, London, 1894, p. 384). (See **N**).

hollowness, Buddha meant the dream-like unreality, the delusive appearance (that is *Māyā*)[1] of all sensible things that make up the Universe. The subsequent translation of *Sunyavāda* into the false Doctrine of Nothingness cannot be ascribed to Buddha himself.[2]

—in religion.

That Buddha was a follower of the Religion of the Upanishads is strikingly brought to light by the words which escaped his lips as soon as he had attained his enlightenment under the famous Bodhi-tree at Buddha-Gaya. In those words, the Vedantic doctrine of the soul as the Creator and of Salvation by realisation of this truth is rehearsed[3] by the Buddha as his own faith. "O maker of the body!" he uttered "I have seen thee ; no more shalt thou

---

[1] See Kumarila Bhatta : Tantra Vartika 81—20. Cf. La Vallée Poussin : " Vedanta and Buddhism " (Journal of the Royal Asiatic Society, 1910, p. 133—134). The Yoga Philosophy of the Hindus also speaks of *Māyā* as *Sunya*. (See the Jnanasankalini Tantra, verse 54). (See **N**).

[2] The term *Nirvana* for salvation in Buddhist literature contributed to produce this false doctrine. The term *Nirvana*, however, is not Buddha's own, but occurs in Pre-Buddhistic Hindu Philosophy, and does not mean annihilation. (See **N**.)

[3] This faith was only a rehearsal, a recitation of an already established truth. It was declared by all the Vedic Rishis and the Purva Buddhas. (See Warren : " Buddhism in Translations," Harvard Series, p. 83).

make bodies unto me."[1] This utterance, which has been a puzzle to the Buddhists,[2] can be understood only by those who are versed in the mysteries of the Hindu Religion, viz., the mysteries of the Upanishads or the mysteries of the Yoga.[3] And even as the Rishis

---

[1] The Dhammapada 11—9. Cf. Monier Williams : "Buddhism," p. 38.   (See **N**).

[2] Cf. Knighton's " History of Ceylon," p. 67.

[3] In the Philosophy of the Upanishads, *ātmadarsana*, or seeing the soul by intuition, is held to be the only way of attaining salvation. (Taittiriya Upanishad 2—1 ; Swetaswatara Upanishad 6—15). (See **N**). Practisers of Yoga will remember that by intense concentration or *Dhyāna*, which Buddha always practised, a supernatural vision may be obtained. The method of obtaining such a vision is known in the Yoga Philosophy as the Shāmbhavi Mudrā and is highly extolled by it as the sure path to salvation. (See Hatha-Yoga Pradipika 4—35 ; Gheranda Samhita 3—59 to 62). (See **N**). These sporadic cases of hallucinations are often very wonderful in their accompaniments and also in their agreement in different individuals. (See James : " Psychology," Vol. II, p. 130). St. Francis of Assisi who beheld Jesus in such a vision, immediately had marks of perforation by nails on his own hands and feet. (Cf. S. Baring-Gould : " Lives of the Saints," Vol. XI, p. 111).

of the Upanishads,[1] Buddha maintained that the
A Niskama-Karmin. proper path to this salvation lay in the combined practice of right knowledge with right action.[2] And, further, he held right action to be that which leads to the complete cessation of all desires ;—the same doctrine of desire-lessness[3] as had been taught long before him by the Yoga-Vāsistha of the Hindus, and also by the Mahabharata, more notably, in the chapters of the Bhagavad-Gita, known as the teachings of the *Niskāma Karma*.

---

[1] Cf. the Isavasya Upanishad, Mantra 2. (See **N**).

[2] In the Dharmachakra-pravartana Sutra, Buddha lays the foundation of the Kingdom of Righteousness on the middle path of life, which ultimately consists of right action and right contemplation. See Rhys Davids : " Buddhist Suttas," p. 147.

[3] The Tanhāvāda (Sanskrit,—Trishnāvāda) or Doctrine of Thirst (or desire) plays the same rôle in Buddhism as in Hinduism. According to Buddhism, desire is the source of creation ; and the Vedas also say : " Desire first arose in it, the primal germ."
(Rig Veda : the Nasadiya Sukta, 10—129—4), (See **N**).

CHAPTER II.

The Hindus themselves followers of the Buddha.

Just as there are evidences to show that Buddha was a product of the World-old Religion of the Vedas and a Hindu himself, so there are evidences to show that his worship was originally carried on by the orthodox Hindus themselves, and that there was no such thing as heterodox Buddhism in the beginning of its career. And the evidences are specially strong as they come from the sacred books of the Hindus, the texts of which are regarded by the Hindus themselves as of universal authoritativeness.[1]

First of all, Buddha is unanimously admitted by the Hindus to be an Incarnation (*Avatāra*)[2] of *Nārāyana* or God, who came to rescue the Kingdom of Righteousness

The Buddha an Avatāra of the Hindus.

---

[1] See the Pamphlet named " Buddha-Gaya Mahatmya."

[2] Matsya Purana 47-247 ; Kalki Purana 2-3-26 ; Vayu Purana, Ekalinga Mahatmya, 12-43 ; 14-39 ; Garuda Purana 86-10 ; Varaha Purana 4-3 ; 113-27 ; Nrisingha Purana 36-29. (For texts and other references, see **N**).

from the hands of the wicked into which it had fallen at that time.[1] And the Buddhists themselves admit that their Buddha is the *Nārāyana* of the Hindus.[2] As such, the Buddha received his worship at the hands of the Hindus, like all the other *Avatāras* ; and there is no doubt about the fact that the original devotees of the Buddha were no other than the Hindus themselves. As usual with the Hindus in matters of devotion, *Moortis* or images (idols) are directed to be made to Buddha, and the directions also are given

And an object of their worship :—by the method of Moortipujā or idolatry.

---

[1] This is the function ascribed to all the *Avatārs* in the Bhagavad-Gita (Ch. 4, verses 7-8). Cf. Bhagavata Purana 1-3-28 ; Garuda Purana 1-149-39 ; Matsya Purana 47-247. (For texts and other references see **N**).

[2] Lalita Vistara Ch. 7 ; and, again, Ch. 15. (See **N**). Cf. Rajendra Lala Mitra : " Buddha-Gaya," p. 6.

It is worth noticing that Kshemendra, who was a professedly Buddhistic author, counts Buddha as one of the *Avatāras* of the Hindus in his Dasāvatāracharitam. (Cf. Foucher :—" Ksemendra : Le Buddhavatara."—Journal Asiatique, Paris, 1892, Serie 8, Vol. XX, p. 167 ff). Other Buddhas existed before this one but none of them was regarded as incarnation of *Nārāyana*. Cf. the Yoga Vasistha, Vairagya prakarana 26-39 ; Mahabharata, Santi-parva 285-32 ; Mahaparinirvana Sutra Ch. 5 ; Lalita Vistara Ch. 12 ; Lankavatara Sutra. (A list of some of the Purva Buddhas is given in Prinsep's " Useful Tables," p. 229). (See **N**).

for these to be with two hands, long ears, seated in deep meditation in the posture called the Padmā-sana of the Yogins, and wearing the two yellow robes of the *sannyāsin*,[1] all representing him as the Hindu ascetic which he actually was in his life-time.[2] And it is expressly stated that these images, made for worship according to the rules of Tantra, are to be worshipped by people of the orthodox Hindu community.[3] As usual in Hindu idolatry, a certain kind of *Sāla-grāma* or Sacred Stone is mentioned as symbolical of Buddha.[4] Further, a special *Tilaka* or mark on the forehead is enjoined on all orthodox Hindus who

by the method of Sālagrā-mapujā or Symbol-worship ; and by Tilakadhārana or carrying a special mark on the forehead.

---

[1] In the line of Hindu " *sannyāsa* " (or asceticism) Buddha was the successor of Dattatreya, and Sankarāchārya the successor of Buddha. (See **N**).

[2] Linga Purana 2-48-28 to 33 ; Agni Purana 49-8 ; Bhavisya Purana, 2-73 ; Hemadri : Ch. 1 of Bratakhanda (the portion dealing with the twenty-four forms of Vishnu) ; Hemadri, Ch. 15 of Brata-khanda. (For texts and other references see **N**).

[3] Suta Samhita 4-3-21 ; and Suta Gita 8-45. (See **N**).

[4] Special Symbols are prescribed for special objects of adoration in the Hindu Shastras. The Symbol special to Buddha is a particular kind of the *Sālagrāma* stone. See Brahmanda Purana. (See **N**).

show a partiality to the Buddha's worship.[1] For them
his worship has also been elaborated by the Hindu
Scriptures themselves into a system consisting of rites

—by Pratah-
smarana

—by Dhyāna

—by Bratapujā

to be observed from morning to evening,
namely, the Buddha-Prātahsmaranam or
early-morning salutation to the Buddha;[2]
the Buddha-Dhyānam or meditation on
him ;[3] the Buddha-Bratapujā or reading

---

[1] Suta Samhita : Suta Gita 8-34. (See **N**).

It should be noted here that the Buddha, like all ascetic
teachers of India used to wear the *Tilaka* and this is proved by
many of his images in stone having the *Tilaka*, which, however, was
a circular one in his case. (See p. 169 ff.) This fact is all the more
confirmed by the Barabudur images of Java having both the *Tilaka*
and the *Yajnopavita* (or the Brahmanical sacred thread) depicted
on them. *Rightly, therefore, is the image of Buddha worshipped by
the Hindus, with the Tilaka put on its forehead.* The Java images,
undoubtedly, reveal a very early state of Buddhism, when it was
not differentiated from Hinduism. (See p. 175 ff.)

[2] Garuda Purana 2-31-35 ; Bhagavata Purana 1-3-24 to 29.
(See **N**).

[3] Agni Purana 49-8 ; Meru Tantra, Avatāraprakarana, 36 .
Sankarāchārya in his hymn to the Ten Avatāras. (See **N**).

his life (or hearing the same recited by another),

—by Gāyatri accompanied by observations of occasional fasts and festivities ;[1] the Buddha-Gāyatri or the Vedic formula of address **—by Mantra** special to Buddha ;[2] the Buddha-Mantra or the incantation proper to him ;[3] and the **—by Namaskārah** Buddha-Namaskārah or the final salutation to the Buddha.[4] Further, the place, Buddha-Gaya, where he attained his **—by Tirtha yatra or pilgrimage to his resorts.** enlightenment, together with the famous Bodhi-tree under which it took place, is regarded as a *Tirtha*, or place of pilgrimage by peoples of the orthodox

---

[1] Agni Purana 16-1 ; Garuda Purana 1-2-32 ; 1-149-39 ; Baraha Purana 211-65 to 66 ; 48-22 ; 49 (the whole chapter) ; Bhavisya Purana 2-73 (twice in the chapter) ; Hemadri, " Bratakhanda " Ch. 15 ; Nirnaya Sindhu, Ch. 2. (For texts and other references see **N**).

[2] Linga Purana : 2-48-28 to 33. (See **N**).

[3] Meru Tantra, Avatāraprakarana, 36. (See **N**). For various mantras of the Buddha see the Tara Tantra. (Barendra Research Society Series, No. 1).

[4] Bhagavata Purana 10-40-22 ; Kurma Purana 6-15, and 10-48 ; Vayu Purana 30-225 ; Baraha Purana 55-37 ; Padma Purana, Kriyākhanda 6-188 ; 11-94 ; Padma Purana, Sristikhanda 73-92 ; Garga Samhita, Viswajitkhanda 13-49 ; Meru Tantra, Avatāraprakarana, 36. (For texts and other references see **N**).

Hindu community. who, according to the injunctions of their own scriptures,[1] flock thither in great numbers to offer *pindas* .or libations to the manes of departed ancestors.

It is held by some European savants that long before the advent of Buddha, the Pippala (or fig-tree) was an object of worship among the Hindus,—that the name Bodhi-tree has always been a synonym for the Pippala, and that Bodhi-Gaya, not Buddha-Gaya, was the original name of the place, derived from this Bodhi-tree and not from the Buddha. Further, on this ground, they contend that the Hindus are enjoined to worship the Bodhi-tree only and not the Buddha in their pilgrimage to Buddha-Gaya.

Some objections answered :—

This view, however plausible it may seem to be, cannot be accepted. Of course, the tree was considered sacred by the Hindus from time immemorial, and the Buddha was all the more a true Hindu for choosing his seat beneath it in his last and most determined act of devotion.[2]

(1) The tree and Buddha.

---

[1] Brihannila Tantra 5 ; Skanda Purana, Abantikhanda 68-30 ; 70-4 ; Vayu Purana 2-49-26 to 29 (also 2-49-31 to 34, found in some Editions) ; Agni Purana 115-37. (See **N**).

[2] The Sacred Fire of the Vedas was produced in the first instance by friction with two pieces of dry wood, preferably the wood from the Aswattha tree. This preference given to the Aswattha (or Pippala) for its wood, led to the tree being regarded as sacred by the Hindus. Buddha's veneration for it confirms him in the Hindu Religion. (See Rhys Davids : " Buddhist India " : p. 231).

As for the term Bodhi-tree being always and every-where a synonym for the Pippala or fig-tree, the assertion is not true. As a synonym for the Pippala, the term occurs only in the Lexicon of Amara Singha[1] who is well-known to have been a Buddhist himself. Pre-Buddhistic literature can produce nothing to corroborate it; and, even up to the present time, no other Pippala tree, whether at Buddha-Gaya or elsewhere has been called by the name of Bodhi-tree except the one which sheltered the Buddha during his reaching the enlightenment. The Lexicon, there-fore, intends the term Bodhi-tree not as a synonym for all Pippala trees but only for that one which had become so famous as to deserve a name in the Lexicon. As for the place Buddha-Gaya, it was formerly known as the " Urubelā-ban," (more correctly, Uruvilva-vana), or the forest of the village named Uruvilva, the modern Urela ;—and it, like the tree, derives its present name very properly from the Buddha who made it known to the whole world.[2]

—the tree derives its name from Buddha.

---

[1] The Amarakosha : 2-42-1.

[2] The old pokhar (or tank) south of the temple, in which, according to tradition, Buddha used to bathe, is called the Buddha-pokhar. It has grown considerably bigger than what it originally was, by mud being dug out of it to build the Temple at a much later date. (See the Imperial Gazetteer of India : " Bengal," Vol. II, p. 50). The tank evidently derives its name from Buddha and there is no dispute in this point. So there is no reason why a dispute should be raised about the names of the tree and the place, and why a different derivation is to be sought for them. According to the Harvard authorities, Bodhi-tree (Bo-tree) means ' any tree under which a Buddha attains the supreme enlighten-ment." (See Warren's " Buddhism in Translations " : p. 499).

Further, the contention that the Hindus are to worship the Bodhi-tree and not the Buddha is also untenable. The Hindu Scriptures expressly lay down that after having **first** worshipped *Dharma* and *Dharmeshwara*, the devotee is **next** to worship the *Bodhi-taru*.[1]

—Hindus to worship Buddha first and the tree next.

The term " Dharmeshwara " in the above passage means Buddha. The Religion of Buddha was known in India as the Dharma ; while Buddha was known as the Dharmeshwara, the Dharmaraja, the Dharmarasi, the Dharmapala, etc.[2] The Lexicon, too,

---

[1] Vayu Purana 2-49-26. (See **N**).

[2] Lalita Vistara, Ch. 7. (See **N**). " Dharma or Dhammo—the former being Sanskrit, the latter Pali—constitutes one of the three grand divisions of the Buddhist faith ; and, in the Pali writings, Buddha himself is often spoken of as Dhammo (Dharma). In the time of Asoka, the common term employed to denote this religion was Dhammo. Dharmeswara, or Lord Dharma, is the Deity who personifies Dharma. If Dharma be regarded as the Buddhist creed, then this appellation would refer to the supposed divine head of such creed, or Buddha."—Sherring : " Benares," p. 85–86 (Ch. V). Cf. the terms Dharma-Mandir, Dharma Bāpi, Dharma Kupa ; and the names Dharma Asoka and Dharmarasi (Sherring, p. 251).

Cf. Paul Carus : " The Dharma : an exposition of Buddhism." (Chicago). Cf. the Buddhist formula of prayer : " I take refuge in the Dharma." (See **N**). [See Waddell : " The ' Refuge Formula ' of the Lamas." (Indian Antiquary, Bombay, 1894 ; Vol. XXIII ; p. 73–76)].

gives the word Dharmaraja as a synonym for Buddha ;[1] and it is well-known that the worship of *Dharma-Thākur*, confined to a sect of the Vaishnavas in some parts of Bengal and other provinces of India, is a form of the Buddha's worship.[2]

The subject of the prohibition to Hindus from going to Buddhist Temples and the allied topic of a Deutero-Buddha may fitly be taken up here.   The text regarded as the authority on this point prohibits Hindus from going to Jaina Temples only[3] (" *na gach-chhet Jaina-Mandiram*":—one should not go to the Temples of the Jainas) ; and the difference between Jaina and Buddhist is well-known.[4] The supposed prohibition arose through a confusion of this text with another which speaks of Buddha as the *Jina-suta* or son of Jina (" *Buddha nāmnā Jina-suta*

(2) The Jaina and Buddhist Temples.

---

[1] Amarakosha : 1-1-1-8 ; Vaijayantikosha : 1-1-33. (See **N**).

[2] This subject has been most ably and admirably brought to light by Mahamahopadhyaya Pandit Haraprasad Sastri (President of the Asiatic Society).

[3] This text is more of an interpolation than of an authority. Its origin can not be traced definitely.

[4] The images in Jaina Temples must, as a rule, be always in the nude state (naked), while the images of Buddha must show him as wearing garments. [Cf. Leon Feer : " Tirthikas et Bouddhistes." Leiden. 1885. (Transactions of the International Congress of Orientalists, part 3, section 2)]. (See **N**).

Kikatesu bhavisyati ":—the *Jina-suta* named Buddha will appear in the lands of *Kikata*).[1] The *son of Jina* is exactly what is meant by the word *Jaina*, and hence, on the first thought *Jaina-Mandir* might be taken to include Buddhist Temples also along with Jaina Temples proper.   But Buddha was the son of Hindu parents of the Kshatriya tribe, and could by no means be called the son of a Jina.[2]   Further, all the texts in which the term *Jina-suta* occurs, do not prohibit the Hindus from going to Buddha's temple, but, on the contrary, enjoin upon them the recollection of Buddha as the first thing to be done on waking up.—(" In the beginning of the *Kali-Yuga*, the *Jina-suta* named Buddha will make his appearance in the lands of Kikata.   In every *Yuga* or Age he comes to restore order among men when the wicked get the upper hand.   He who, every day morning and evening, reverentially recites his birth-story is freed from all afflictions."[3]   " In the dawn of the *Kali-Yuga*, the *Jina-suta* named Buddha will make his appearance in the lands of *Kikata*.   From him has sprung up all this creation.   He is to be reverentially worshipped with all sacred

—Hindus prohibited from the f o r m e r only.

---

[1] See below, p. 37 ; p. 41.

[2] See above : p. 8.

[3] Bhagavata Purana : 1-3-24 to 29.   (See **N**).

rites and observances."[1] "The wise should always recollect the names of the ten *Avatāras* including Buddha."[2]) Hence some other meaning for the term *Jina-suta* is to be sought for. According to the Lexicon "Medini," which is regarded as a first-class authority, another synonym for the word *Jina* is *Bhagavān* or God (*Bhagavān nā Jine*).[3] On this authority, the term *Jina-suta* would mean the son of *Bhagavān* or God, that is to say an incarnation of *Nārāyana*,—an *Avatāra*,—which the Buddha is admitted on all hands to have been.[4] And this must be taken to be the

—Jina-suta is not Jaina.

---

[1] Garuda Purana : 1-2-32.   (See **N**).

[2] Garuda Purana : 2-31-35.   (See **N**).

[3] The Medinikosha :—(ta-endings, § 215. For *Jina* in the sense of Vishnu (or God) see also Hemachandra 2—130 ; Halayudha 1-25 (and Aufrecht's Glossary, p. 222) ; St. Petersburg Dictionary (s. v.) ; Sabda Kalpa Druma (s. v.).   (See **N**).

[4] See above, p. 25 ff.   Another name for Vishnu or *Bhagavān* (God) is *Jishnu* which comes from the same root as Jina and means the same thing, viz., the conqueror or Lord.   (See **N**).   Sometimes the words Jina, Jinendra and Jaitra are applied to Buddha, not with any sectarian significance, but only in the sense of "the victorious," the mighty.   In the Vaijayantikosha of Yadavaprakasa the word *Jina* has been mentioned twice separately, once as the epithet of Buddha, and again as the epithet of Arhat or **Tirthika** of the Jainas. (Oppert's Ed., p. 5).   In the St. Petersburg Dictionary, " Jina-putra " is taken to mean " Bodhisattwa."   It may also mean " successor of the Buddhas of old,"—the word " Jina " meaning Buddha.—(Amarakosha 1-1-1-8 ff.)

real meaning of the term in the texts containing it,—especially as those texts themselves contain additional passages which bring out and corroborate this meaning, e.g.—" In every *Yuga* (or Age) he comes to restore order among men when the wicked get the upper hand ; " " From him has sprung up all this creation." And these passages are precisely those which are understood to have reference to an *Avatāra* alone. The term *Jina-suta* thus meaning an *Avatāra* and not a Jaina, the text which prohibits the Hindus from going to the Jaina Temples cannot be taken to mean the Temples of *Jina-suta* or Buddha.

The theory, proposed by some,[1] of two contemporary Buddhas,—one for Hindus and the other for Buddhists,—is altogether fanciful. The plural number in the word *Kikatesu* in all the texts about *Jina-suta* (e.g., " *Buddha nāmnā Jina-suta Kikatesu bhavisyati*,"—the *Jina-suta* named Buddha will be in the **lands** *of Kikata*), is very significant for this point. A man cannot be born in a plurality of places at one time. Hence the word " bhavisyati " (i.e., will be) in the said texts does not refer to Sākya Singha's birth but refers to his beginning his career after having

(3) The theory of Buddha and a Deutero-Buddha exploded.

---

[1] Prinsep : " Indian Antiquities," Vol. II. (Useful Tables, p. 164) ;—Prof. Wilson in the Oriental Magazine for 1825 ;—Patel's Chronology. (See **N**).

assumed to himself the name of Buddha.[1] And those texts therefore mean as follows : The Incarnation of God (*Jina-suta*) born at Kapilavāstu, will, after he has assumed his title to Buddhahood (*Buddhanāma*), make his appearance[2] (*bhavisyati*) in a plurality of places in the land of Kikata (*Kikatesu*),—the land which he will choose as the play-ground of his activities.

Of this Buddha, who is the ninth *Avatāra* of the Hindus, it has been said that he confirmed the atheists in their own atheistical views (*Sammohāya suradvishām*)[3] ; knowing that atheists were sufficiently punished in their own atheism, the intolerable burden of which would inevitably lead, by reaction, to theism.[4]

The full story of Buddha's assuming the functions of a beguiler and the purpose achieved thereby is given

---

[1] Cf. Lalita Vistara, Ch. 25 ; (p. 400 of Lefmann's Ed., line 19) :—" The good people hear the Dharma in the lands of Magadha (*Magadhesu*)." *Magadhesu* here (also in the plural) is the exact equivalent of *Kikatesu* in the texts referred to above (See **N**). Note also that just as the birth-day of Buddha (or *Buddha-Jayanti*) is held to be the day on which he attained his Buddhahood (or Enlightenment), so his birth-place is held to be the place where he attained his Buddhahood, that is, Buddha-Gaya, in the land of Kikata. The Hindus regard the attainment of gnosis as a new birth ; cf. the term " *Dwija* " or twice-born (for a Brāhmana, i.e., one who has knowledge of Brahma).

[2] See Rajendralala Mitra : " Buddha-Gaya," p. 6.

[3] Bhagavata Purana 1-3-24 ; Garuda Purana 1-2-32 ; the same 1-149-39. (See **N**).

[4] Cf. Suta Samhita : Brahma Gita, Ch. 4,—verses 66, 67, 70 (See **N**).

in the authoritative Hindu work called the Vishnu Purana.[1]   The Nārada Pancha-rātra also puts it thus : " Buddha fascinated the ideas of the atheists by the doctrine of Universal Nothingness ; he thus beguiled them away from the Vedas, and, by so doing, preserved the Vedas from destruction and interpolation at their hands.   He gave to all exactly according to their deserts.   He preserved the Vedas for the good of the believers, while confirming the atheists in their own atheistical philosophy."[2]   The Tantrasāra says that to deprive the wicked of their strength, Buddha devised the apparently irrefutable doctrine of Nihilism.[3]   In the Lalita Vistara occurs the following : " He put an end to all troubles by taking up the doctrine of Nihilism and of the consequent Non-existence of the Soul."[4]   It should be noted that Buddha based his doctrine of Nihilism for the atheists upon texts of the Vedas which apparently have a Nihilistic meaning, but really have their bearing upon the Vedic doctrine of *Māya*.[5]   On this count, he has been called

---

[1] Vishnu Purana 3-18-15 ff.   (See **N**).

[2] Narada Pancha-ratra, 4-3-156 to 159.   (See **N**).

[3] Tantrasāra, Ch. 4 ; in the hymn to Vishnu, verse 9.   (See **N**).

[4] Lalita Vistara, Ch. 12.   (See **N**).

[5] Cf. Rig Veda Samhita :—10-72-2 ;   10-129-7.   Chhandogya Upanishad :—6-2-1 ;   Taittiriya   Upanishad :—2-7.   Cf.   the Sariraka Bhasya :—2-4-1.   (See **N**).

a deluder (*Māyin*) ;[1] and some have even gone so far as to suppose that his religion and worship are therefore prohibited to Hindus. This supposition, however, is a wrong one. Instances of doing good to the world by practising a trick of delusion upon the wicked are not uncommon in the Hindu Shastras, and the deluder in such cases is never put under ban and bar for doing that.[2] Not only Buddha but all the other *Avatāras* also are known to have practised delusion upon others, thereby beguiling them in some point to their detriment, while securing some good to the world.[3] In the Bhagavad-Gita, Krishna, as the incarnation of the Deity says : " From me come both presence of mind and correct knowledge, as well as forgetfulness, that is to say, both correct guidance and leading astray."[4] And the Upanishads also declare the same thing thus,—

---

[1] Kurma Purana :—10-48 ; Bhagavata Purana :—10-40-22 ; also Mahabharata : Bhismastavaraja in Santiparva. (See **N**).

[2] An instance of leading astray by a false doctrine is given in the Devi Bhagavata (Book IV, Ch. 10 to 13) ; another instance of creating weakness and bringing ruin through inculcating a false doctrine may be found in the Matsya Purana, 24-37 to 49. (See **N**).

[3] Siva Purana, Rudra Samhita, Kumarakhanda :—9-25 (See **N**).

[4] Bhagavad-Gita : 15-15. (" Apohana " being taken in the sense of absence of mind, oblivion, or putting out of wits). (See **N**).

" It is God Himself Who makes one do the right thing whom He wishes to elevate. It is God Himself Who makes one do the wrong thing whom He wishes to hurl into ruin."[1] Hence the supposition that Buddha is under a religious ban to the Hindus for preaching a false doctrine to the atheists is unsupportable ; especially as the texts which describe him as the deluder of the wicked do not disparage him on that account but enjoin his worship all the more for that.[2] The Buddha who preserved the Vedas from the hands of the atheists by diverting them into another doctrine,[3] is verily the one and the same personality who is to be worshipped with all due honours and ceremonies by the Hindus also, according to the authority of their own sacred codes. This refutes the theory of a Deutero-Buddha proposed to explain the existence of Nihilistic teachings in Buddhism, which is supposed to be otherwise inexplicable. The Prince Sākya Singha who was born at Kapilavāstu as a Bodhisattwa (or one destined to

---

[1] Kaushitaki Upanishad :—3-9. (See **N**).

[2] Bhagavata Purana 1-3-24 ff ; the same 10-40-22 ; Garuda Purana 1-2-32 ; the same 1-149-39 ; Kurma Purana 10-48 ; Vayu Purana 30-225. (See **N**).

[3] Cf. Bhagavata Purana 6-8-17 ; Garuda Purana 202-11 (See **N**).

become a Buddha) was the one who afterwards ripened into his Buddhahood in the land of Kikata, where he went from place to place[1] diffusing the light which he had received for the benefit of all believers, without entering into disputations with the atheists and others who opposed him.[2] Just as Rāma, born at Ayodhya, had his mission in Lanka ; or Krishna, born at Mathura, had his mission in Kurukshetra ;—so Buddha, born at Kapilavāstu, had his mission in Kikata. This land of

---

[1] [Cf. Waddell : " Discovery of Buddhist Remains at Mount Uren in Monghyr district, and Identification of the site with a celebrated Hermitage of Buddha." (Journal of Asiatic Society, Bengal, 1893, Vol. LXI, p. 1-24)].

[2] " Sakya spent his whole life in diffusing his doctrines, —he seems never to have formally embodied his followers into a sect."—Scenes in India (Oriental Annual) 1835, p. 240. Buddha followed a liberal and enlightened policy in preaching his doctrines. He never entered into anything that seemed like a religious disputation and did not oppose those who opposed him. His method was the method of persuasion and tolerance. He admitted into his order even those who differed from him. It is well-known that he allowed a sect called the Sthaviras to grow up within his system and respected their teachings as well as their teacher, whom he · called Sthavira Subhuti. (See **N**.) Subhadra, a Bhiksu whom he initiated into his doctrines, was an opponent of him up to the end of his days. It is even known that Devadatta, one of his disciples living with him, was so much opposed to him in theory and practice that he even made attempts on the life of his master, who always would forgive and put up with him. (See p. 16 above).

Kikata subsequently received the name of Bihar from the extraordinary number of monasteries (called *Vihāras* in the native tongue) which sprang up there when Buddhism had its day.[1]

Another erroneous supposition is that the land of Bihar was long under the sway of Foreign Buddhists. The supposition has its root in the word Magadha, which is another name for the province of Bihar,—and which is wrongly supposed to have been derived from the Maugs or Burmese, who, in their turn, are supposed to have governed it. The word Magadha, however, as a name of Kikata or Bihar, is derived from the large number of Magas, a sect of Brahmanas (called also Sākadwipins), who lived exclusively in that province. As a proof of this it may be pointed out that the name Magadha was current before the time of Buddha as

(4) Magadha never owned Buddhist sway.

---

[1] As has been pointed out by Vincent Smith and others, there was no such thing as Buddhist period in the history of India. All the great Buddhist kings of India were Hindus worshipping Buddha. (See **N**).

the proper name for the province which subsequently came to be called Bihar.[1]

This erroneous supposition is also partly due to travellers' tales relating to the village of Gaya in Tibet (perhaps somewhere in the Gyantse region of Tibet). This Tibetan village of Gaya was hostile to the interests of the Lamas and Chinese ;[2] and this hostility produced the notion that it was a Hindu habitation under Buddhist sway,—which notion brought about, by confusion, the supposition that the Indian Gaya was once under the sway of Foreign Buddhists, especially as both the Gayas resembled each other in their castle-like buildings.[3]

---

[1] Lalita Vistara Ch. 25 ; Mahabharata, Bhismaparva : 11-36 ; Vishnu Purana : 2-4-69 ; Samba Purana : 16-87 to 88 ; Padma Purana, Swargakhanda, Ch. 8, verses 33 to 34. (See **N**).

[See the St. Petersburg Dictionary, s. v. Maga (and Mriga) ; and cf. Wilford : " Asiatic Researches," Vol. IX, p. 32].

[2] " Huc's Travels " : Book II, Ch. 9, pp. 282-284.

[3] Gandhola was the old Indian title of the Buddha-Gaya Temple. At Gyantse in Tibet is a Gandhola which is a model of the Buddha-Gaya Temple transplanted to Tibet. See Waddell : " Lhasa and its Mysteries ", p. 229 (cf. O'Malley : " Gaya," p. 52, note). An exact model of the Great Temple exists in Burma also. The Bawdi Paya at Pagan in Burma takes its name from the Bodhi-tree at Buddha-Gaya, and is an exact reproduction of the Great Temple of Buddha-Gaya. (Ferrars : " Burma," 2nd Ed., p. 33).

(44)

As regards Buddha-Gaya, it has always been in Hindu hands. The Ceylon Bhikshus who lived in the Temple were Hindus of the Buddhist (or, more properly, the Vaishnava) sect. In 1795, the Hindus owned it; and a little later, a mission from *Tamasā-dwipa-mahā-amarāpurā-pāigu*, sent by *Mahā-dharmarāja*, found it completely in the hands of the Hindus.[1] " The Hindu *Sannyāsis* have held the place for over five centuries."[2]

---

[1] Hamilton: " Ruins of Buddha-Gaya ; " 1823 ; p. 1.

[2] Record by the Government of Bengal in the Buddha-Gaya Temple Case of 1894 ; p. 32.

CONCLUSION.

The Buddhists a sect of Hindus ejected by them.

The original Religion of Buddha was thus part and parcel of the orthodox Hindu system based upon the World-old Religion (Sanatana Dharma) of the Vedas. Nay, more than that, the Hindu Scriptures themselves say : " Those who understand the Vedas will see that of all the religions which have their roots in the Vedas, the religion mixed up with the Tantric form of the worship of Buddha is the one which surpasses the others in excellence."[1] It would appear that the original worship of Buddha was an idolatrous Tantric worship of his image with repetitions of incantations to him, carried on by a sect of Hindus specially devoted to him,[2] having points of

Evidences of Buddhism having been originally incorporated in Hinduism :—

---

[1] Suta Samhita : 4-20-16. (See **N**). Cf. La Vallée Poussin : " On the authority of Buddhist Agamas." (Journal of the Royal Asiatic Society, London, 1902, p. 374 ff).

[2] Cf. Burney : " Discovery of Buddhist images with Deva-nagari inscriptions at Tagoung, the ancient capital of the Burmese Empire.' (Journal, Asiatic Society of Bengal, 1836, Vol. V, p. 157 ff). Even in the present times, the worship of Buddha as carried on in foreign countries bears a close resemblance to the Hindu methods of worship which strikes the minds of travellers. " The walls of the (Buddhist) temples (at Pekin) were covered with Sanskrit inscriptions and pictures of mythological subjects.......... The whole ceremony possessed a good deal of similarity to the performance of our Hindu ritual."—Maharaja Sir Jagatjit Singh of Kapurthala in his " Travels in China, etc., " p. 34-35. See Crawfurd's remarks on the purely Indian character of all the great sculptural and architectural monuments of Buddhism in Java. Also Barrow's remarks to the same effect in his Travels in China. Numberless Buddhist remains have been mistaken for Brahmanical, by antiquaries and even by the natives. See Oriental Quarterly Magazine, No. XVI, pp. 218-222. (Quoted from Hodgson's Essays, p. 67).

difference with the other Hindu sects,[1]—in the same manner as the worship of Rāma or of Krishna is represented by a sectarian division which is devoted to the one or the other, but which is none the less within the pale of orthodox Hinduism for that. Its Tantric character up to the present time is borne out by its employment of incantations (or *mantras*

---

[1] Cf. Max Muller,—" Buddhism originally a Brahmanic sect" (Anthropological Religion, Gifford Lectures, p. 34).

The points of difference which originally distinguished Buddhism were not such as would require its expulsion from Hinduism ; such points arose at a much later period and were not intended by the founder. (Rhys Davids,—" Buddhism," 1910, p. 84).

It may be noted here that the later works on Buddhism disclose a greater diversity of sects within it than the earlier ones. There are evidences that Christian tenets found their way into some sects of the Buddhists. (See the life of Tsong-ka-pa in " Huc's Travels," Vol. II, Ch. 2, esp. p. 51). A parallel to the Christian Saint who was " never guilty of washing his feet " is to be found in the Buddhist sect of the " Apagata-pada-mrakshana " (those who never washed their feet). (See **N**). But even in the life-time of Buddha differences of opinion existed among his followers. (See above, p. 41, foot-note 2). And it was for this reason that soon after Buddha's death, two meetings of the Buddhist Bhikshus took place, viz., one at Rajagriha, the other at Vaisali. The former fixed the canon exactly as it was delivered by the Buddha ; the latter expunged everything that digressed from the fixed canon. See the Cullavagga (Kulavarga), Books XI and XII. [Cf. Sandor Csoma Korosi : " Different systems of Buddhism : from Tibetan Authorities " (Journal of the Asiatic Society, Bengal, 1838, Vol. VII). Cf. also David : " The Buddhism of the Buddha and Modernist Buddhism " (Buddhist Review, 1911, Vol. III, p. 18)].

(It may be remarked here that even in the Vedas there are different Sākhās or Recensions by different Rishis belonging to the same Samhitā-School).

e.g., "**Om Mani Padmè Hum**," etc.), by its acknowledging the efficacy of amulets (called *Kavachas* by
the Hindu Tantriks), and by its constant association
with the worship of the goddess Tārā, one of the leading
deities of the Tantras of the Hindus.[1]

The Hinduistic origin of Buddhism is decidedly
proved by some of the images of Buddha
(1)—External evidences. having the *Bara* (boon) and the *Abhaya*
(no-fear) in the two hands,[2]—a design

---

[1] The Buddhists believe in a Creative Power, the *Sakti* of the
Hindus,—and, like the Hindus, worship it in the female form of
personification. This is the goddess Tārā, also called Kāli by
Hindus,—the Kurukullā of Buddhists and Hindus alike. (See
Jaske's Tibetan Dictionary, p. 3 ; and Āgamavāgisha's Tantrasāra,
the chapter on Shyāmāpujā). Most of the Buddhist Temples have
some vestiges of Tārā also. This took rise, most probably, from
Buddha's hymn to Transcendental and Infinite Wisdom which he
personified as a goddess, " Bhagavati Prajnā Pāramitā-amitā."
(See the Introduction to the Astasahasrika). (See **N**). Tārā,
holding the lotus (*padma* or *utpala* flower), is no other than the
Hindu goddess of that name and description. Bodhidharma,
Asanga, etc., who introduced Buddhism into China and other lands,
were Hindus, as is proved by the three horizontal lines on the
forehead depicted in all their images.

[Cf. Tārā Tantra which is a Buddhistic work, and Sragdharā-
Stotra, which is a Buddhist hymn to Tārā. See also Blonay's
" Buddhique Tara ; " and Waddell : " Tara " (Journal of the Royal
Asiatic Society, 1894, p. 63). As for the " Mani Padmè " formula,
see Francke :—" The meaning of the ' Om mani padmè hum'
formula " (Journal, Royal Asiatic Society, 1915, p. 397-404) ; see
also Monier Williams : " Buddhism," p. 373 (note) ; Koeppen's note,
" Brahmanism and Hinduism," p. 33 ; Knight's " Cashmere and
Thibet," p. 369. As for the amulets, see Carte: " Notice of amulets
in use by Buddhists " ; also Csoma's Remarks on the above.
(Journal of the Asiatic Society, Bengal, 1840, Vol. IX, p. 904 ff).]

[2] Agni Purana : 49-8. (See **N**).

altogether meaningless and unintelligible to all except those versed in the mysteries of the Hindu Religion.[1]

---

[1] In Vedic Mysticism, it is declared that the Sacred Fire can make the gods visible to the naked eyes. (See Rig Veda Samhita, Khila Suktas 28-6). (See **N**). It is said that when a god actually appears in the Fire, he holds up one hand in the manner of saying "no fear" to the devotee, while with the other he seems ready to offer some boon to the same. This attitude distinguishes the real god from hallucinations. The Hindu *Yogins* hold that by meditation of a god in this attitude one can make him assume this attitude and receive from him a boon (*bara*) and a blessing (*abhaya*). In the Brihannaradiya Purana (Ch. 2, ver. 39), it is said that *Yogins* behold in their Yoga the Buddha in this attitude. (See **N**). These images of Buddha were, therefore, made by the Hindus; for the Hindus alone believe in the said Mystic doctrine. Other forms of images, too, namely, those representing the Dhyani Buddhas in the various postures of *Padmāsana* (sitting with legs crossing each other), of *Nāsāgradristi* (eyes fixed on the tip of the nose), or of *Prānāyāma* (breath held in suspension),—all answer to the directions given by the Yoga and Tantra of the Hindus for carrying on the process of meditation. All this, undoubtedly, tends to prove that originally the Hindus began the worship of the Buddha in their own way. Even the Barābudur at Java contains Buddha's images of this Barābhayada description,—as pointed out by Foucher in his "Beginnings of Buddhist Art," p. 256. (See also Karl With : "Java," plates 9-12).

The *Mudrās*, or postures of the hands, shown in the images of Buddha, were all strictly Hinduistic *in their origin*. Cf. Burgess : "Buddhist Mudras" (Indian Antiquary, 1897, Vol. XXVI, p. 24). For plates of *Mudras*, see Hoffmann : "Nippon Buddha Pantheon." Cf. Frankfurter : "The Attitudes of the Buddha." (Journal, Siam Society, Bangkok, 1913, Vol. X, part 2, pp. 1-35). [Marco Polo speaks of the origin and spread of idolatry outside India through Buddhism. (See pp. 317-319 of Vol. II of Cordier's Edition of the Travels,—Book III, Ch. 15.) Cf. the Islamic term "Boot" for idol, and "Boot-kādoh,"—Pagoda,—for Buddhist Temple, probably derived from "Boot," the Muhammadan name of Buddha. (Cf. Prinsep's "Useful Tables : " p. 229 of Vol. II of his Antiquities)].

The temples to Buddha were mostly erected by the Brahmanical followers of Buddha, the expenses being borne by kings of the same type. All the authorities concur in saying that the Great Temple at Buddha-Gaya was erected by a Brahmana, perhaps by Amara-deva, about the year 300 A.D.[1] That Brahmanical kings worshipped Buddha is proved by the fact that the coins of the Yaudheya kings of India have a Brahmanical inscription on one side and the images of the Chaitya and the Bodhi-tree on the other.[2] These coins, also, belong to the period about 300 A.D.;[3]— whence it seems probable that Amaradeva erected the Great Temple through the munificence of his royal patrons.

Apart from these external evidences got from comparative researches, there are stronger proofs for the point at issue,—proofs furnished by a critical study of the Religion itself. To any one who makes even a

---

[1] Ferguson : " History of Architecture," Vol. I, p. 77 ; Cunningham : " Mahābodhi," p. 21 ; Rajendralala Mitra : " Buddha-Gaya," p. 243.

Amaradeva, the Brahmana, has been wrongly taken by some to be Amara Singha, the author of Amarakosha, another devotee of Buddha, who was a Kshatriya (and a Hindu as well).

[2] Cunningham : " Coins of Ancient India," pp. 75 to 78 (and Plate 6, Figure 9). The inscription reads : " Bhagavato Swāmino Brāhmana Yaudheya." (See **N**). The word Chaitya means the Buddha's place of worship. (See p. 10, above).

[3] Cunningham : " Coins of Ancient India," p. 76.

4

superficial study of Buddhism, the whole thing, taken as a complete system by itself, would seem to be inadequate or defective in many salient points. Buddhism deals

(2)—Internal evidences.

with moral precepts mainly, and even these moral precepts are not so much intended for householders as for ascetics (or monks). It is a code of Monastic Ethics, in which questions concerning the sanctity of marriage, the responsibilities of the individual, the obligations of society, the mutual duties of subjects and kings, the problems of God, of free-will and of immortality,— questions which any complete religious system must take cognizance of,—are passed by altogether or treated with an apparent indifference.[1] It cannot be argued that Buddhism professes indifference to these questions ; for, as Kant has said, it is vain to profess indifference to those questions to which the mind of man can never really be indifferent.[2] The whole thing, however, becomes clear when it is understood that Buddhism originally was only a reformation of Hinduism. Buddha set himself only the task of reforming the corruptions which had crept into

---

[1] This point was suggested by Dr. B. M. Barua in his Lectures at the Dharmarājika Vihāra of the Bauddhacharya Dharmapala Cf. Vāchaspati Misra,—Tātparya-tika, p. 300 ff. (See **N**).

[2] Quoted by James Seth in the Problem of God,—p. 391 of his " Ethical Principles."

Hinduism, especially into the then existing Hindu asceticism and priestcraft :[1] but he never undertook to change the whole face of that religion. Beyond his own province of reformation, Buddha retained everything of Hinduism, not only by the consent implied in his silence and want of criticism, but also by the open method of quotations and references to the Hindu Scriptures as his authority.[2] Buddha, therefore, did not ignore those vital questions of religion, but meant them to be retained just as they are in the main religion of the Hindus to which he himself belonged. It is well known, too, that Buddha gave preference to Brahmanas and Kshatriyas among his disciples,[3] and that he confirmed the sacramental character of marriage and disapproved of widow-marriages and promiscuous marriages. All these, undoubtedly, bear testimony to his propagation of true Hinduism.

---

[1] The Hindu ascetics of those days were the followers of Dattātreya, the Gymnosophists or naked philosophers of the Greek invaders under Alexander the Great. It is in reference to them that Buddha says, " Not nakedness nor platted hair can purify a mortal who has not overcome desires." (Dhammapada 10-13). His opposition to Brahmanism (or priestcraft) is brought out in the Brāhmanavarga of Dhammapada, while the term " Bho Gautama " with which he was accosted derisively by the Brahmans evidently shows their hostility to him.

[2] See above, p. 17 ff.

[3] See the Sutta Nipat 2-7. Cf. Coppleston : " Buddhism," 2nd Ed., p. 141 ; and Rhys Davids : " Buddhism," 2nd Ed., p. 84.

In course of time, however, the Hindu worshippers of Buddha began to admit foreigners within their sect ; and then followed a series of sectarian struggles with the orthodox community,—of priestly oppositions,[1] of doctrinal attacks,[2] and, finally, of regal and authorised persecutions,[3]— which ended not only in Buddhism being regarded as a degenerate and heterodox religion but in its totally disappearing from the native soil of India, leaving only feeble traces here and there.[4] But although Buddhism in its

Buddha and Buddhists. Ejection of Buddhists from Hinduism :— (1)—Real cause of ejection.

---

[1] For example, those of Bhatta Kumarila Swamin.

[2] For example, those of Acharya Sankara Swamin.

[3] For example, those of Shashānka, the king of Karnasuvarna. [It is doubtful whether the Buddhists were ever persecuted by the Hindus. Sankara, however, never persecuted the Buddhists,—his chief contention being with the Ritualistic School of Brahmans represented by Mandana Misra.—See " Buddhism in its Relationship with Hinduism," by the Bauddhacharya Dharmapala, p. 11].

[4] The worship of Dharma, Dharmarāja, Dharma-Thākur, Dharma-Vaijayanti, etc., prevailing in some of the lower classes of the Hindus is a survival of this degenerate form of Buddhism. [Cf. Haraprasad Sastri : " Buddhism in Bengal since the Muhammadan conquest." (Journal of the Asiatic Society, Bengal ; 1895, Vol. LXIV). For unavowed, veiled, or crypto-Hindu Buddhists, see Nagendranath Basu,—" The Modern Buddhism and its Followers in Orissa." As for the survival of Buddhism in India, and for Dharma-worship, see the Census of India, 1901, Vol. I, part 1, p. 369-371].

degenerate condition was thus ejected by Hindus, yet Buddha has never vacated the throne which he still continues to occupy in the hearts of all the Hindus, nay, of all humanity.[1] Buddha sat enthroned in the heart of Sankarāchārva[2] who caused all the true followers of Buddha to give up their sectarian denominations and return again to the World-old Religion of yore.[3] Afterwards Buddhism was newly

---

[1] Cf. Rhys Davids,—" Buddhism," p. 85.

[2] Compare Sankarāchārya's own declaration in his Dasāvatāra-stotram (or hymn to the Ten Incarnations) :—" The Buddha, the Prince of Yogins, the living Buddha, dwells in the centre of my heart." (See **N**).

[3] It is pretty certain that Sankarāchārya persuaded most of the Sramanas to become Sannyāsins, and caused the Vihāras to relapse into Mathas. In this way the original Buddhism became absorbed into Hinduism, and the nominal sect of the Buddhists vanished from India. Even now many of the tenets of the original Buddhism may be found promulgated in the various sects of the Hindu Vaishnavas, who worship Buddha also in their worship of Vishnu and his ten incarnations. " Vaishnavism clearly reflects the influence of Buddhism. The most important shrines of the Vaishnavas of Bengal are in the keeping of the Brahmans who are themselves strict Sāktas." (Census of India, 1901, Vol. I, Pt. I, p. 361). Cf. Stevenson : " On the intermixture of Buddhism with Brahmanism in the Religion of the Hindus of the Dekkan." (Journal of the Royal Asiatic Society, London, 1843 ; Vol. VII). The ten incarnations including Buddha are worshipped in Cooch Bihar, Nepal, Kashmir, etc. The " Nepal Mahatmya " even says that to worship Buddha is to worship Siva.

systematised by Nāgārjuna in India and by Padmapāni outside India.[1] Being now degenerate and prevalent among aliens and foreigners only, to whom it is practically confined, Buddhism is wrongly supposed to have been anti-Vedic in its origin. On this supposition

(2)—Supposed cause of ejection. rests the erroneous notion that Buddha was ejected out of Hinduism, together with his religion, for speaking against the Vedas. True, Buddha spoke against the Vedas; but he spoke against only that portion of the Vedas which advocated the slaughter of animals and had degenerated into a religion of elaborate rituals and outward formalities.[2] Now, as regards the said portion of the Vedas, it has been denounced before him by other

---

[1] Padmapāni, the formulator of " Om mani padmè hum," is also known as Avalokiteshwara (or, in Biblical language, one who has had the vision of the Ancient of Days). Nāgārjuna is not admitted by all to have appeared as yet. The new systematization was thoroughly Tāntric in its character and gave rise to the modern Buddhist Tantras, which, strangely enough, are accepted by Hindus also. A sect of these Buddhist Tāntrikas regards the Hindu Deity, Siva, as Avalokita and his consort as Tārā " the Saviouress." (See Taranath's " History of Buddhism," Ch. 10. Cf. the Article by Waddell in the Journal of the Royal Asiatic Society, London, 1894, pp. 51-89). (See **N**).

[2] Padma Purana, Kriyakhanda : 6-188 ; Bhagavata Purana : 11-4-22 ; Sankara Vijaya : 12-8 ; Gita-Govindam :—Hymn to the *Avatāras*. (See **N**).

portions of the Vedas themselves and by the Bhaga-vad-Gita ;[1] and, after him, also by Sankarāchārya himself.[2] Therefore, if these last mentioned are not to be regarded as heterodox, Buddha alone cannot be so regarded for a fault which was common to them all. The fact is that orthodox Hindus never forgive anyone who presume to contradict anything of the Vedas, and hence there are passages in the Hindu writings themselves against Sankarāchārya himself.[3] The following occurs in the Padma-Purana. " The great doctrine of *Māyā* (that is Sankara's Philosophy) appears to be an interpretation of the Vedas but really is

---

[1] Mundaka Upanishad : 1-2 (the whole chapter) ; Gough : " Philosophy of the Upanishads," p. 102 ; Bhagavad-Gita, 2-42 ff. (See **N**).

[2] Sankara's mission, as exhibited in the Sankara Vijaya, was to substitute asceticism for ritualism. His chief contention was not with the Buddhists, as is wrongly supposed by many, but with Mandana Misra, the chief advocate of the Ritualistic Philosophy of that time, whom he defeated in argument and converted into his own views. As for the Buddhists, they were, on the whole, representatives of asceticism ; and Sankara found no difficulty in converting them. His dispute with the Buddhists was only with a sect of them who stood in his way and who rather misrepresented the original teachings of the Buddha.

[3] See Jaya Chandra Sarma's Article on Buddhism in the Sahitya Samhita, 1309 (Bengal **Year**), No. 9-10.

anti-Vedic. It has been proclaimed to the world to hasten its destruction. This doctrine of *Māyā* is a false philosophy ; verily, it is Buddhism in disguise. It has been preached by the Destructive Power in the guise of a Brahmana of the Kali Age (namely, Sankarāchārya).[1] But, although thus disparaged for having dared criticise a portion of the Vedas, Sankarāchārya was never ejected out of Hinduism for that. On the contrary, up till now he has always been regarded as one of the foremost of the leaders of orthodox Hinduism based upon the World-old Religion of the Vedas. In like manner, and equally with Sankarāchārya, Buddha was disparaged for having raised his voice against a portion of the Vedas, but he was never ejected from Hinduism for having done that. The cause of the ejection of his followers is due to reasons which developed in his religion, as has been already said, at a later time long after Buddha had passed away.

Buddha has never been ejected by Hindus :— the Buddhists have been. Very properly, therefore, it might be held that not Buddha but the Buddhists only, as they stood at a later time, were the thing that was ejected by the

---

[1] Padma Purana. (Quoted by Vijnana Bhikshu in his commentary on the Sānkhya Philosophy). (See **N**).

Hindus.[1] And authorities, too, concur in this as well as in all the other points detailed above, as shown below.

" Primitive Buddhism is only to be gathered by inference from the literature of a later time. Buddha did not array himself against the old religion. The doctrines were rather the outgrowth[2] of those of certain Brahmanical schools. His especial concern was salvation from sorrow. It passed away in India not from Brahmana persecution but rather from internal causes,

Authorities quoted: —Dr. Smith

---

[1] In an inscription of the tenth century, it is distinctly stated, that a Buddhapada or Buddha's foot was set up at Buddha-Gaya expressly for the purpose of performing thereon the Hindu rite of Srāddha. (See Charles Wilkins's translation of the Inscription, —Asiatic Researches, Vol. I, p. 284). Whatever may be the real date of this inscription, it undoubtedly proves that Hindus had never ejected Buddha from the pale of their Vedic Religion, and, consequently, that Buddha himself was strictly a follower of the Vedic Religion. " Had pure Vedism been the faith of the people, there would have been little need for a Buddha." —Sewell : " Early Buddhist Symbolism " (Journal of the Royal Asiatic Society, London, 1886, p. 365).

[2] Cf. " The marks of its derivative character are stamped on every portion both of its faith and practice ;—its creed can be deduced from Brahminism by logical sequence."—Scenes in India, (or Oriental Annual), for 1835, p. 236.

such as relaxed discipline, overgrowth of monasticism, etc.''[1]

" Atheism is certainly not the common teaching of all Buddhists, for a sect among them acknowledge a self-existent Deity whom they call Adi Buddha.[2] Nor do they positively deny the existence of the soul. It is impossible to charge

—Rev. Dr. K. M. Banerji.

---

[1] Smith :—Cyclopædia of Names (Article " Buddha "). Undoubtedly, Buddhists were persecuted by the Hindus, especially during the reign of King Shashānka. [Cf. Rhys Davids : " Persecution of the Buddhists in India." (Journal of the Pali Text Society of London ; 1896). Also cf. Journal of Asiatic Society, Bengal ; 1854, p. 472 ; and Sherring's " Benares," p. 268-270]. But mere persecution can never be the cause of the disappearance of any religion. The Buddhists were *not* persecuted by the Hindus more than the Hindus have been persecuted by the Muhammadans through unending ages ; and yet the religion of the Hindus is still perfectly intact. The decline and **fall** of Buddhism in India must therefore be ascribed to causes other than mere persecution, for persecution too often strengthens a faith rather than destroy it, as the history of Christianity shows. The effect of persecutions, especially of those by Muhammadans, was to put a stop to the influx of Buddhist Foreigners coming to India to visit the Temple and other places of their pilgrimage. (History of the Temple, in Journal of the Mahabodhi Society, Vol. XXIX, No. 9 ;—Anagarika H. Dharmapala).

[2] Cf. Wright : " History of Nepal " (Buddhist Recension), Chapter I. [Cf. the name of a sect of Buddhists, viz., Sarvāstivādins, (or All-believers) (Pali Text Society Journal, 1904-1905, p. 67, London).]

them with positive denial of the soul in the face of their declarations of future retribution.[1] The sceptic, they say, will be born in hell or as a beast. The wise man will be born in a Devaloka or as a man.[2] As to their reviling of the Veda, it would be more correct to say that they ignore rather than revile, its contents."[3]

" Buddha himself as represented to us in the canonical writings of the Buddhists shows no hostility to —Max Muller. the Brahmans in general nor does he seem to be fond of arguing against Brahmanism. Though Buddhism is a reaction against Brahmanism, there is an unbroken continuity between the two. Buddha does not argue against the Vedic gods. He tolerated them in that subordinate capacity in which they were tolerated by the authors of the Upanishads."[4]

---

[1] The final unification of consciousness with will is a state of **perpetual peace or Nirvana** which is the Buddhist's immortality. Cf. Bigelow : " Buddhism and Immortality " (Ingersoll Lecture, 1908) ; also cf. Paul Carus : " Karma and Nirvana. Are the Buddhist doctrines nihilistic ? " (Monist, Vol. IV, 1893-94, p. 417-439. Chicago). Cf. Sen : " Buddhism and Vedantism,—a Parallel " (Journal of the Bihar and Orissa Research Society, 1918, Vol. IV, p. 141 ff).

[2] Cf. the Chhandogya Upanishad : 5-10-7. (See **N**).

[3] Rev. Dr. K. M. Banerji, LL.D.,—" Dialogues on Hindu Philosophy," Dialogue 5.

[4] Max Muller : " Collected Lectures," Lecture 3, pp. 94-95. In his earlier works, the scholar had not come to this conclusion. (See **N**).

" Hinduism, therefore, was contained in the Dharma of Buddhism and the great object of Gautama's advent was not to uproot the old religion but to purify it from error and restore it."[1]

—Monier Williams.

" Buddha can hardly be said to have intended to found a new religion. He was unwilling to discuss questions concerning the nature of God or the soul, the infinity of the universe, and so forth, holding that such discussions are unprofitable. Without formally denying the existence of Almighty God, the Creator, he ignored Him."[2]

—Vincent Smith.

" Buddha was seeking a way of deliverance. He

---

[1] Sir Monier Williams : " Buddhism," p. 206. In the Tvishya Jātaka, the study of the Vedas is recommended with the practice of the Dharma as the true Buddhism of the householder. (See Sarat Chandra Das : " Indian Pandits in the Land of Snow ; " p. 87). So in several Buddhist works, as Brihad Dharma Purana, etc., it is mentioned that a time of degeneration will come when the Buddhists shall cease to regard the Vedas. This admits that it is the duty of Buddhists to regard the Vedas.

[2] Vincent A. Smith :—" The Oxford History of India ; " p. 54-55. Cf. " Buddha nowhere denies an Infinite First Cause " (" Prajnā Pāramitā-amitā"—in the Introductory hymn to the Astasahasrika);—Waddell : " Buddha's Secret " (Journal of the Royal Asiatic Society, London, 1894, p. 384).

found that deliverance in self-culture and self-discipline.

He busied himself little with metaphysical speculations as to the origin of evil and of sorrow. What he desired was to make it possible for man to rise superior to the delusions and the desires that produced this evil and this sorrow.

—Dr. Gottheil.

" Buddha and his doctrines suffered defeat, and that, all along the line. It is true that no moral system, no religious doctrine, no philosophic theory can remain for long as pure as it was at its source. Accretions from the outside are added to changes from within, so that its latter view is very different from its former aspect. But nowhere has that change been more complete than it has in Buddhism. The Buddha had been cryptically silent in regard to the Super-sensual side of faith : he had affected to ignore it as being in no connection with his own teachings, and as unnecessary to furnish the basis for his system of ethics.[1] Yet, human nature refused to be cheated of its longings. It felt in Asia—as it has always felt—that the call to a moral life sounds hollow and vain unless it is fortified by some authority that is extra-(or rather, supra-)

---

[1] For the true explanation of this silence, see above, p. 50.

human ; and that, detached from connection with the general scheme of the universe, the aspirations of mankind cannot be held at the level at which the Buddha wished to keep them. What nearer and better course was there for his followers than to satisfy their cravings by turning the Buddha himself into a divinity? Gradually this belief made its way, and changed Buddhism from a code of ethics into a religious organization."[1]

"One misconception is the prevalent notion that Gautama was an enemy to Hinduism. **—Rhys Davids.** This is not the case. Gautama was born, and brought up, and lived, and died a typical Indian. He had but little quarrel with the religion that did prevail. His purpose was to build it up, to strengthen it, not to destroy it. The differences (between him and other teachers) are probably much more apparent now than they were then, and by no means deprived him of the support and sympathy of the best among the Brahmins. Many of his chief disciples, many of the most distinguished members of his Order, were Brahmins. Neither Gautama nor the great body of the Brahmins believed the two systems to be

---

[1] Dr. Richard Gottheil, Ph. D. (Director of the New York Public Library), in the Bulletin of the Library, 1916, Vol. XX, p. 114.

incompatible then. We hear of no persecutions till long after the time of Asoka, when Buddhism had become corrupt ; and Buddhism grew and flourished side by side with the orthodox belief. So far from showing how depraved and oppressive Hinduism was, it shows precisely the contrary. Gautama's whole training lay indeed outside of the ritualistic lore. His teachers had renounced the sacrifices. He was the greatest, and wisest, and best of that long line of reformers who have endeavoured to infuse new strength into the religious life of India."[1]

" Buddhism has developed into contradictory systems in different countries, while in India it changed greatly even during the first ten years of its existence. The Buddhists are indebted to Brahmans for almost all of their speculations and even in the choice of names, such as *Dharma*, *Nirvāna*, etc. As pointed out by Dr. Weber the word " *Buddha* " (or Prati-buddha) in the sense of a man who had attained to perfect knowledge of Self, first occurs in the Satapatha Brahmana of the Vedic literature (14-7-2-17).[2] Gautama's adherence to

—Elizabeth A. Reed.

---

[1] Rhys Davids : " Buddhism (Non-Christian Systems)," p. 83-85.

[2] Cf. Brihadaranyaka Upanishad : 4-4-13. (See **N**)

Brahmanic ideas is repeatedly shown in his teachings. He had a way, however, of clothing old ideas in a new dress, which proved very attractive to his followers. His sympathy with much of the teachings of the Upanishads was very strong. In its earliest phase Buddhism was not a religion; but merely a system of philosophy. The doctrines of Buddhism have found their origin upon Indian soil and in the earlier creeds of the Hindus. The principal theories of Buddhism lived in India long before Gautama's time. He took the thoughts of the few and promulgated them among the many. Although he did not wish to abolish caste as a social institution still he disregaded the exclusiveness of the priests and addressed himself to all classes, and hence Buddhism was a reaction against Brahmanism even while retaining much of its faith."[1]

It has been said before that Buddha was not much given to fighting with his opponents, and that he often confirmed the atheists in their own views as the best way of converting them into theism.[2] But even when

---

[1] Elizabeth A Reed :—" Primitive Buddhism," pp. 25, 183 ff, 198 ff, 204.

[2] For true explanation of this fact see above, p. 37 ff. Even the Sautrāntikas, themselves a sect of Buddhists, maintain that Buddha when teaching the *Sunyatā* (or Nihilism) was directed by principles of conciliatory policy (*Upāyakaushalya*).—See La Vallée Poussin : " On the authority of Buddhist Agamas " (Journal of the Royal Asiatic Society, London, 1902, p. 374, foot-note).

doing so, Buddha did not deny the existence of the Godhead, but only relegated it to the domain of the unknown.[1] Hence it has been said :

—Gough.

"Buddhism is the Philosophy of the Upanishads with the Brahman left out."[2] Moreover, escape from sorrow was according to him the problem of life,[3] and he found its complete solution in the moral system which he founded upon the Doctrine of Desire-lessness[4] without raising the problem of God. And this, precisely, is the position taken up by the Yoga-Vāsistha Mahārāmāyana of the Hindus which purports to be the teachings of the Vedic Rishi named Vasistha imparted to his royal pupil, Rāma, the grand-predecessor of Buddha in the line of the *Avatāras*. As one of the writers on this point says :

—Viharilala
Mitra.

"The resemblance between the teachings of the Yoga-Vāsistha and those of Buddha is so close that even the Buddhists are led to

---

[1] As a specimen of Buddha's Agnosticism, see the Tevigga (Trivijna) Sutta (in the Buddhist Suttas translated by Rhys Davids). [Cf. Costa :—" Buddhism, an agnostic religion." (" Buddhism ": Rangoon, 1905, Vol. II, p. 79)].

[2] Gough : " Philosophy of the Upanishads," p. 187.

[3] " Buddha set himself the task of solving the mystery of life in order to find the Way of escape from continual Becomings, which was clearly involved in Misery."—Waddell : " Buddha's Secret " (Journal of the Royal Asiatic Society, London, 1894, p. 372).

[4] In Buddhism, Tanhā (Trishnā or thirst) is the name of desire.

identify Rāma with Buddha,[1] and regard the Yoga-Vāsistha as a classical work of the Buddhists."[2]

Now, to bring the whole thing to its proper and natural conclusion, Buddha proclaimed that he had discovered the Path to Salvation, and he exhorted all people to be their own lights on the path.[3] And, just at the time of his final passing away, he spoke to his favourite disciple, Ananda, saying that the true Path to Salvation consists not in worshipping the Buddha with hymns and offerings but in devoutly fulfilling all the greater and the lesser duties of life,

Conclusion :— The Will in Buddhism.

---

[1] Cf. Fausboll : " The Dasaratha-Jātaka, or the Buddhist story of King Rāma " (Kopenhagen, 1871).

[2] Viharilala Mitra, the translator into English of the Yoga Vāsistha, in his fragments called " Mitra-Rahasya." (See his " Secrets of the Law : " Ch. I, § 2, p. 7). (The author of the Yoga-Vāsistha is said to be the same as that of the Rāmāyana, **viz.**, Vālmiki).

[3] Mahaparinirvana Sutra, Ch. 2, § 33. This, undoubtedly, demands the exercise of the will-power by regular acts, e.g., by prayer and devotion. The term " negation of the will," as used in Buddhism, is a misnomer : it should be " negation of desires." The negation of desires is not negation of the will, but rather the highest effort of the will-power,—the salvation-bringing act, the last action without further reaction,—which sets the Spirit free from the impositions of matter and mind. (Mukti, Nirvāna, Excelsior, Perfection). (See **N**). " Buddha's Metaphysics appears to be based on Will. Schopenhauer indeed admits the affinity of his theory with Buddhism." [See Waddell : " Buddha's Secret from a sixth century commentary " (Journal of the Royal Asiatic Society, London, 1894, p. 382). Cf. Mrs. Rhys Davids : " On the Will in Buddhism " (Journal of the Royal Asiatic Society, London 1898, p. 47) ; Cf. also Mrs. Rhys Davids : " On the Culture of the Will in Buddhism " (Transactions of the International Congress of Orientalists ; Paris, 1899,—Section I, p. 143 ff.)].

and that this alone is not only the worthiest homage due to Buddha, but also is the worship of him in the form most desired by him and, therefore, most acceptable to him.[1] This lands us at once on the ground of the World-old Religion of the Vedas and its prescribed duty. (See Introduction above). For, of all the duties of human life, the duty of stepping into the next higher stage of evolution is the highest, the most ancient, original and universal, as well as the most incumbent on mankind, inasmuch as it is productive of the greatest good and includes all the other duties within itself.[2]

Thus it has been established that Buddhism, as part and parcel of Hinduism, came out from the World-old Religion of the Vedas and into it returned.[3]

---

[1] Mahaparinirvana Sutra, Ch. 5, § 6. (See **N**).

[2] The Black Yajur-Veda 1-5-10-2 ; Taittiriya Brahmana 2-4-3-3. Cf. the Mahābhārata : Rajadharma, 8-37 ; 60-52. Cf. Sankarāchārya's last advice to his disciples : " Always study the Vedas and carefully perform the one duty enjoined by them,"— (in the Sādhana-panchaka). The subject has been fully discussed in a separate work entitled " The First Book of the Upanishads." (See **N**).

[3] Journal of Bihar and Orissa Research Society, Vol. IV, p. 143.

**May this be acceptable to the Buddha
as the unmeaning prattle of a child to its mother.**

Dedicated to my Buddhist brothers all over the world.

Written at Buddha-Gaya and laid at the Master's feet on the eleventh day of November, 1922 A.D.

YOGIRAJA'S DISCIPLE MAITREYA.

APPENDIX.

The Doctrine of *Ahinsā* or Non-hate in Buddhism.[1]

The word " Hinsā " signifies the slaughter of a
living being. To slay requires an unsympathetic
attitude of mind towards the victim, and this, in
positive term, is called hatred. " Hinsā," therefore,
means hatred,—that narrow mood of mind habitual to
vulgar people who take for dead all whom they do not
like.[2] Hence its opposite, " Ahinsā,"
Ahinsā :—its real import. means non-hate,—absence of hatred :
that is, in positive term, sympathy or love. (Schopenhauer : " Ueber das Fundament der Moral," §18.)[3]

It has been held by some that absence of hatred
is the height of religion (*Ahinsā paramo dharma*),[4]
inasmuch as it promotes love which is the power of
uniting the individual souls with one another, the power
of restoring the lost Paradise. Others have maintained that hatred has its undeniable *raison d' etre*

---

[1] This has reference to pp. 18-19 above (and to the foot-notes
therein).

[2] See James : " Principles of Psychology," Vol. I, p. 312.

[3] Cf. Weber's " History of Philosophy," p. 553.

[4] Mahābhārata : 1-11-13.

(or right to be) in the fact that it is the force of righteousness,[1]—the force which enables the individual to live his life upon Earth. Philosophy upholds the principle of righteousness as the basis of the kingdom of *moral* restraint, while Religion upholds the principle of love as the basis of the kingdom of *beautiful* freedom. This is the conflict of Philosophy and Religion,—of justice and forgiveness, of utility and beauty ; and herein are to be found the roots of all the contradictions of life, and of all its dire tragedies. The conflict of justice and forgiveness often seems so pronounced that some have even looked upon *charity as the negation of morality*.[2] It must, however, be admitted by all that love is the force of attraction ; and, as such, it is

---

[1] Righteousness implies hatred towards wrong. In the never-ending fight of good against evil, hatred shall always retain its place. There is a world of thoughts in the old adages : " Sparing the wicked is killing the virtuous " ; " Let him who loves peace prepare for war." The poet sings the same thing thus :—

> " Yes !   maugre all thy dreams of peace still
> must the fight unfair be fought ;
> Where thou mayst learn the noblest lore
> to know that all we know is nought."

—(The Kasidah of Abdul Yezdi, translated by Burton).

[2] E.g.,—Huxley, in his " Prolegomena to Evolution and Ethics " ; p. 32. Cf. Mahābhārata, Rajadharma : 15-49. (See **N**).

the chief factor in the process of the withdrawing *of the many* individual souls *into the one* Supreme Soul, the Original Cause, the Godhead of creation. Further, it is a fact of common experience that hatred retards the natural development of both the mind and body of the hater, while love makes them both bloom forth in their natural splendour in the lover. Hatred is like a fiercely burning fire, which makes heated, it is true, all who happen to come near it, but consumes the very heart and core of the thing wherein it rages.[1] Love, on the other hand, is like the cool moon-shine which illumines but scorches not,—"a luminary which shines all the brighter for the darkness which surrounds it,—the light which lightens every man that cometh upon Earth". Truly, hatred is the canker of the human breast, the underminer of health, beauty and happiness,—an insane delirium in itself. As one who, taking a fancy to see some one object in the colour of red wears a pair of red glasses, must perforce see all objects in that colour: so the mind that entertains hatred towards an enemy cultivates bitterness towards the whole universe. To this culture of hatred there is no antidote except the practice of love ; and the practice of love, if it is to end in universal love, must begin with love to an enemy. The old teaching that hatred will be quenched

---

[1] Cf. Vidyaranya Swamin : Jivanmukti-Viveka, Ch. 2. (See N).

as soon as due revenge is taken,[1] has been found to fall short of its purpose ; for hatred, like all other passions, grows by feeding upon victims. Buddha means this when he says : " Hatred does not cease by hatred at any time ; hatred ceases by love : this is its nature."[2] True it is that forgiveness is often a masked form of fear ; and a more despicable creature than the weak, timid saint cannot be imagined. All the religions of the world therefore inculcate hatred towards wrong,[3] and even Buddhism represents the gods and goddesses as armed with weapons to defend the right.[4] But, provided that it is not prompted by motives of weakness, love has its *raison d' etre* as much as hatred has its. People who are prone to hate would be the best workers of the world if the fire of their hatred were quenched and their energies set free for nobler undertakings.[5] To quench this fire of hatred,

---

[1] Life for life, tooth for tooth, etc.   (Bible : Exodus xxi, 24).

[2] Dhammapada 1-5.

[3] The Vedas say : " God adjusted hatred towards the false " (White Yajur-Veda 19-77 ; Taittiriya Brahmana 2-6-2-3). Cf. Bible : Amos v, 15 ; Job xl, 11 ff.—Koran : Surah 22, ver. 40. The same thing is advocated by the Gita and the Durga of the Hindus, and also by all the great Epics of the world, e.g., the Rāmāyana, Mahābhārata, Iliad, etc.

[4] Cf. Socrates : " If the Rulers of the universe do not prefer the just man to the unjust, it is better to die than to live."   (See James Seth : Ethical Principles, the Problem of God, p. 421).

[5] To them may be applied what Shakespeare says in his sonnets :

> " Some fierce thing replete with too much rage,
> Whose strength's abundance weakens his own heart."
> " Making a famine where abundance lies,
> Thyself thy foe, to thy sweet self too cruel."

love must be invoked to play its part. Viewed in this light the practice of love,—religion in its truest sense,—is higher than the teachings of philosophy ; and the rule of " Ahinsā," or unconditional and absolute forgiveness, higher than all the austere laws of morality.[1]

The Doctrine of " Ahinsā " (non-hate) or " Viswa-prema " (universal love), is the highest teaching of all the religious teachers of the world.[2] Buddha is sometimes wrongly supposed to have been the original propounder of this doctrine, which, in its turn, has therefore been wrongly supposed to have been anti-Vedic in its origin and significance. In fact, however, it existed in the World-old Religion of the Vedas from time immemorial.[3] But, undoubtedly, the best expression has been given to it by the Founder of Buddhism who based his love on complete self-sacrifice.

The doctrine is Vedic in its origin and Buddhist in its perfection.

---

[1] Mahābhārata, Udyogaparva 33-48ff ; and Dronaparva 198-59. (See **N**). Cf. Pascal : " The interval which is infinite between body and mind represents the infinitely more infinite distance between intellect and charity." (Cf. Adams : " Secret of Success ", p. 222).

[2] Cf. Laotzu : " Requite injury with kindness " ; and Christ : " Love your enemies."—(Legge : " Texts of Taoism," Vol. I, p. 92 ; and Bible : Matthew, v. 44). [Cf. Smith : " The Christian and Buddhist conceptions of love " (Buddhist Review, London : 1909, Vol. I)].

[3] See above, p. 19 and notes thereon. Cf. Rig Veda 6-48-10 ; Sama-Veda 2-974 ; the Isavasya Upanishad,—6. (See **N**). The term " Ahinsā " occurs also in the *Yoga Sutras* of Patanjali, 2nd Pāda, 30th Sutra. For Morality in Buddhism and Vedanta, see Paul Dahlke's " Buddhist Essays," translated by Bhikshu Silachara, p. 148.

Thus does he enunciate it : " Knowing his own guilti-
ness (or *karma*) a man can easily bear his sufferings at
the hands of others as the mete retribution of his own
acts ; but him I call the true saint who, armed with
the strength of unshakable forgiveness, submits to the
extreme penalties of the fetters and the gallows without
the least feeling of hatred towards his enemies, *although
fully conscious of his own perfect guiltlessness.*"[1] The
mellow tone of this all-forgiving love pervades the
whole range of Buddhistic literature,[2] and fills its
melodies with a sweetness that is redolent of the
days of innocence and artless simplicity.[3] No wonder,
therefore, that Buddhism found its way to the Poles
and the Antipodes ;[4]—for, erring humanity everywhere

---

[1] Dhammapada : 26-17. (See **N**).

[2] E.g.,—the stories in the Avadāna- kalpalatā. [Cf. Lloyd :
" Buddhism, the Religion of Love." (Buddhist Review : London.
1910, Vol. II). [Cf. Dr. Wilson : " Cave-temples of Western
India," Ch. 9, § 2 :—" A common designation of Buddhism on the
cave inscriptions being ' the religion of mercy ' "].

[3] Cf. the " Thera-Gāthās " and the " Theri-Gāthās."

[4] Cf. Holmboe : " Traces of Buddhism in Norway before the
introduction of Christianism." (Paris). Also cf. Alphonse Germain :
" Buddhism in ancient Mexico, according to recent discoveries "
(Etudes Franciscaines ; Paris ; 1905 ; Vol. XIII). The Saint
Josephat of the Christians or Yudasatf of the Arabs is the same as
the Bodhisattwa (Buddha). [Cf. the story of Barlaam and Josaphat
by John of Damascus ; and see Liebrecht's " Jahrbuch "].

The Sacred Maya Stone of Mexico, however, is not Buddhistic
in its origin ;—Maya being the name of the dialect in which an
inscription on the stone was written. So also Guatemala does
not derive its name from Guatama ;—the word " gua " meaning a
" place " as in Nicaragua, Antigua, etc. [See the " Sacred Maya
Stone of Mexico," by Dr. Parry. In the History of Guatemala by
Don Juarros a different derivation is also given].

stands in need of forgiveness and restoration to love,
—of that mercy by which it lives and for which it cannot
but make the way. So the greatest of the world's
poets also has sung : " The quality of mercy is not
strained. It is twice blessed ; it blesseth him that gives
and him that takes. It is an attribute to God Himself ;
and earthly power doth then show likest God's when
mercy seasons justice."[1] The discovery of the way
to this kingdom of love and the establishment of it
within one's self is one of the highest achievements of
man's genius and free-will in combination. This is the
perfect way, the finding of Buddha, the finding of Christ,
the finding, in short, of the Divine in the human.

And herein does Philosophy join hands with
Religion,—producing its own logical reasons to support
the dogmatic command of the latter to love one's
enemies. For, if life is understood to be no more than
a self-created dream, then one should naturally cease
to hate the enemy he has created unto himself ;[2] but if
life is to be taken as real and earnest, then one should
by all means preserve himself from hatred, which is the

---

[1] Shakespeare : Merchant of Venice (Act, iv, sc. 2, l. 184 ff).

[2] This is the teaching of the Upanishads. (Cf. Isavasya
Upan. 6). Shakespeare makes a near approach to it when he says :—

> " If we shadows have offended
> Think but this, and all is mended,
> That you have but slumbered here
> While these visions did appear.
> And this weak and idle theme
> No more yielding but a dream," etc.
> —(A Midsummer Night's Dream : 5-254 ff).

most prolific cause of madness, murder, suicide, remorse,—of ruin of body and wreck of mind.[1]

The word *Dharma* or Religion, by its very derivation, means that which holds together. The Universe is held together by the law of attraction, and love is the highest form of this attraction, inasmuch as it is the conscious form. Therefore love is the highest religion, and this establishes the truth of the saying : " *Ahinsā paramo dharma.*" (See Postscript on p. 148 ff.)

---

[1] " Plato says very finely that a man should not allow himself to hate even his enemies : because, says he, if you indulge this passion on some occasions, it will rise of itself on others ; if you hate your enemies, you will contract such a vicious habit of mind as by degrees will break out upon those who may be even your friends or those who are indifferent to you. I might here observe how admirably this precept of morality, which derives the malignity of hatred from the passion itself, not from its object, answers to that great rule which was dictated to the world a thousand years before the philosopher wrote ; but instead of that I shall only take notice with real grief of heart that the minds of many good men among us seem soured by paltry principles, and alienated from one another in such a manner as seems to me altogether inconsistent with the dictates either of reason or religion." (See **N**).

THE BUDDHA=MIMANSA.

<hr>

[N.B. The Pages refer to the First Part of this work and the
Notes refer to the foot-notes therein indicated by a " See N."]

<hr>

NOTES.

Page 1. (Introduction).

Note 1.   Buddha-charita of Aswaghosa, 1-1 :—

श्रियं पराद्धां विदधद्विधातृजित्
तमो निरस्यन्नभिभूतभानुभृत् ।
नुदन्निदाघं जितचारुचन्द्रमाः
स वन्द्यतेऽर्हन्निह यस्य नोपमा ॥

Note 2.   Sully's Human Mind, Vol. II, Appendix,
p. 369 :—

"Both the mental and the material
........are conjoint attributes of one
and the same substance."

Green's Prolegomena to Ethics, Article 33 :—

"Our conception of an order of nature,
and the relations which form that order,
have a common spiritual source."

Page 2.

Note 1.   Brihadaranyaka Upanishad, 4-5-6 :—

" आत्मा वा अरे द्रष्टव्यः श्रोतव्यो मन्तव्यो निदिध्या-
सितव्यः । "

[P. 2 (cont.)]

Mundaka Upanishad, 2-2-5 :—

" तमेवैकं जानथ आत्मानमन्या वाचो विमुञ्चथ अमृतस्यैष सेतुः ॥ "

Note 2. Chhandogya Upanishad, 6-1-3 :—

" येन…अविज्ञातं विज्ञातं (भवति) । "

Brihadaranyaka Upanishad, 4-5-6 :—

" आत्मनि…विज्ञाते इदं सर्वं विदितम् ॥ "

The Bible references :—

" There is a spirit in man." (Job xxxii, 8);

" The spirit of man is the candle of the Lord." (Proverbs xx, 27);

" And the spirit shall return unto God." (Ecclesiastes xii, 7);

" God is a spirit, and they that worship him must worship him in spirit." (John iv, 24);

" In the spirit he speaketh the mysteries." (I Corinthians xiv, 2).

Note 3. In the Religion of the Avesta, Ahura Mazda is the pure spirit (Brahma of the Vedas); Spenta Manyus is the element of light or knowledge (pure mind, Iswara); Angra Manyus is the element of darkness or ignorance (the impure mind, Maya). This element of ignorance has the power of

imagination (Druj, *lit.* deceit) inherent in
it, which is the Will or creative power of
the spirit.

Page 3.

Note 2. The Taittiriya Upanishad (2-8) mentions,
among others, the following classes of
gods, viz., Gandharvas, Pitris, the Ājāna-
jas, the Karma-devas, the Devas proper,
etc.

And the Brihadaranyaka Upanishad,
4-3-33, mentions (among others) the Jita-
loka-devas, the Brahmaloka-devas, etc.

The Bible (Daniel vii, 10 ff.):—

". . . . The Ancient of days did sit, whose
garment was white as snow. . . . . Thousand
thousands ministered unto him and ten
thousand times ten thousand stood before him."

The Koran references:—

Surah 13-12: "Each hath a succession
of Angels before him and behind him,
who watch over him by God's behest."

Surah 16-2: "By His own behest will
He cause the Angels to descend with the
Spirit on whom he pleaseth among his
servants."

Surah 35-1: "Praise be to God, Maker

of the Heavens and of the Earth! Who employeth the Angels as envoys."

Surah 42-50, 52 : "It is not for man that God should speak with him but by vision, or from behind a veil : or, He sendeth a messenger to reveal, by His permission, what He will : for He is Exalted, Wise! Thus have we sent the Spirit (Gabriel) to thee with a revelation, by our command."

Surah 2-91 : "Say : Whoso is the enemy of Gabriel—for he it is who by God's leave hath caused the Koran to descend on thy heart, the confirmation of previous revelations—shall have God as his enemy."

Surah 42-52 : (Just quoted above).

Surah 53-1 : "The Koran is no other than a revelation revealed to him : One terrible in power taught it him, endued with wisdom" (i.e., the Angel Gabriel).

Page 4.

Note 1.   *Cf.* Rig Veda (the opening) :—

"अग्निमीडे पुरोहितम् ।" I salute fire the spiritual guide.

Mahabharata, Banaparva, 200-13 :—

"नावं वेदमयीं कृत्वा तारयन्ति तरन्ति च ।"

[P. 4 (cont.)]

The same, Santiparva, 327-50 :—

"स्तुत्यर्थमिह देवानां वेदाः स्रष्टाः स्वयंभुवा ॥"

Purport:—The religious sentiment has evolved from the knowledge of the existence of higher spheres first revealed by the Sacred Fire.

Note 2.   The Bible references:—

Fire is the symbol of the Deity in the Bible. God appeared to Moses in Fire at the burning bush, and on Mount Sinai. (Exodus iii, 2; xix, 18).

"And there came a fire out before the Lord and consumed upon the altar the burnt-offering and the fat; which when all the people saw they shouted and fell on their faces." (Leviticus ix, 23–24).

"We have heard his voice out of the midst of the fire: we have seen this day that God doth talk with man." (Deuteronomy v, 25).

It was the "hallowed fire" so originated which was kept up without ever being extinguished as the only fire for purposes of devotion, so long as the worship of the Tabernacle was faithfully maintained. (Leviticus vi, 12–13).

[P. 4 (cont.)]

This supernatural fire was renewed at the dedication of the Temple by Solomon (II Chronicles vii, 1), and at the restoration of God's worship among the ten tribes by Elijah. (I Kings xviii, 38 c/ also I Kings xix, 12 : "And after the fire a still small voice").

When the Altar was moved from place to place, the burning embers were taken from it and carried in some vessel kept for the purpose. (Numbers iv, 13).

God showed himself to Isaiah, Ezekiel, and John in the midst of fire. (Isaiah vi, 4–5 ; Ezekiel i, 4 ; Revelation i, 13–15).

It is said that He will so appear at His second coming. (II Thessalonians i, 8).

The descent of the Holy Spirit was denoted by the appearance of lambent flames or tongues of fire. (Acts ii, 3).

Daniel says: "A fiery stream issued, and came forth before Him" (the Ancient of Days). (Daniel vii, 10).

And He led His people Israel through the desert under the form of a pillar of fire. (Exodus xiii, 21).

Note 4. The word Seraphim in Hebrew literally means "burning beings." (Isaiah, Ch. vi)

[The belief in the affinity of spirits to fire is prevalent among the Europeans also. See Frazer's Golden Bough, Vol. II, p. 232.]

Mahabharata, Banaparva, 261-13 :—

"तेजसानि शरीराणि भवन्त्यत्रोपपद्यताम् ।" etc., etc."   The context will show that it refers to the gods, and speaks of them as having fiery bodies, with super-human attributes.

Aniruddha's commentary on the Sankhya Philosophy (5-112) :—

"सूर्यादिलोके तैजसः शरीरः ।"

Rig Veda, 9-113-4 :—

"लोका यत्र ज्योतिष्मन्तः ।"

(Cf. Sariraka Bhasya, 1-2-24 : "अग्निशरीरा वा देवाः ").

Page 5.

Note 1.   Rig Veda, 1-1-2 :—

"स देवाँ एह वक्षति ।"

The same, 1-12-1 :—

"अग्निं दूतं वृणीमहे ।"

(Also in Sama Veda, 1-3 ; White Yajur Veda, 22-17 ; Black Yajur Veda, 2-5-8-5 ; Atharva Veda, 20-101-1).

The same, 1-22-10 :—

"आ या अग्न इहावसे होतां यविष्ठ भारतीम् । वरूत्रीं धिषणां वह ॥"

[P. 5 (cont.)]

Purport :—The Sacred Fire will bring down upon the earth not only the gods, but with them the goddesses also.

Note 2.　Rig Veda, 1-140-1 :—

"वेदिषदे प्रियधामाय...प्र भरा योनिमग्नये ।"

The same, 3-5-7 :—

"आ योनिमग्निर्घृतवन्तमस्थात् ।"

It is worth noticing that there is no mysticism in shaping the vessel of the burning Ghrita into the Yoni-like triangular figure. The reason for doing so is that drops falling from above produce concentric circular waves on the burning Ghrita which upset and gradually put out the fire if the containing vessel is a circular one. But when the vessel is a triangular one, the circular waves strike and break against the sides of the vessel before they could reach the corners ; and thus the three corners, left perpetually burning, maintain the heat necessary to prevent the fire from going out. This was the original cause which led to give preference to the triangle-shape for all Kundas or places of the Sacred Fire.

[P. 5 (cont.)]

Atharva Veda, 3-12-8 :—

"पूर्णो नारि प्र भर कुम्भमेतं घृतस्य धाराममृतेन संभृताम् ।"

Rig Veda, 4-58-5 to 8 :—

"एता अर्षन्ति...घृतव्रजाः...घृतस्य धाराः ।"

"एते अर्षन्त्यूर्मयो घृतस्य मृगा इव ।"

"घृतस्य धाराः...भिन्दन्नूर्मिभिः पिन्वमानः ।"

"अभि प्रवन्त समनेव योषाः...अग्निं घृतस्य धाराः ।"

Purport:—A continuous flow of drops of melted butter was kept up above the Sacred Fire; the height was regulated by the length of a series of one hundred drops (5); the drops kept chasing one another like deer flying from the archer (6); the drops kept gushing out and looked bigger as they descended (7); the drops pressed down the flame of the fire as a loving wife, with her face smiling upon her husband, presses him down.

This method of feeding the fire is known to other Religions also. *Cf.* The Magus, by Barrett, Book 2, Part 2, p. 87: "The two olive trees distilling holy oil into the lamps that burn before the face of God, mentioned in Revelations." (Bible: Zechariah iv, 3, 11–14; Revelation xi, 3, 4).

Perhaps the system of threading a

series of one hundred separate beads on the string for counting incantations (Mālā-japa) had its origin in the hundred-drops regulation of the flow of Ghrita (Satabraja).

Page 6.

Rig Veda, 10-108 : The Story of Saramā and the Panis, especially Mantra 11 :

"Let the Panis (perhaps, Pan-worshippers) go away to a great distance";

"दूरमित पणायो वरीयः ।" They had begun their depredations as early as the time of the Rig Veda.

Mahabharata, Banaparva, 228-5 :

"रुद्रमग्निम् उमां स्वाहाम् प्रदेशेषु महाबलम् ।
यजन्ति पुत्रकामाश्च पुत्रिणश्च सदा जनाः ॥"

The same, 229-27, 31 :

"रुद्रमग्निं द्विजाः प्राङ्ः ।"

"रुद्रस्य वह्नेः स्वाहायाः यस्यां स्त्रीणाश्च भारत ।"

Purport :—Rudra, the Lingam, is Agni or Fire, and Umā his wife, the Yoni, is the "power of producing the gods" (the Swāhā or libation of Ghrita to the Fire).

The term गोवृषध्वजः (one whose ensign is cow and bull) applied to the Lingam (Siva) has its proper meaning when the Lingam is understood to be the symbol of the Sacred Fire, which depends solely on

[P. 6 (cont.)]

cow's butter.   See Mahabharata, 229-27 ;
and *cf*. Rig Veda, 10-5-7 :—

"असच्च सच्च परमे व्योमन् दक्षस्य जन्मन् अदितेरुपस्थे ।

अग्निर्ह नः प्रथमजा ऋतस्य पूर्व आयुनि ऋषभश्च धेनुः ॥ "

Also, "उपेदमुपपर्चनमासु गोषूप एच्चताम् ।   उप

ऋषभस्य रेतसि उपेन्द्र तव वीर्ये ॥ " Rig Veda,
6-28-8.

Note 1.   The following is a specimen of a comparative study of the Bible and the **Rig Veda**.
The Bible says:—

"And it shall come to pass in that day,
that a man shall nourish a young cow,
and two sheep; it shall come to pass, for
the abundance of milk that they shall
give he shall eat butter."

"And an high way shall be there, and
a way, and it shall be called the way of
holiness; the unclean shall not pass over
it; the way-faring men, though fools, shall
not err therein. They shall obtain joy
and gladness, and sorrow and sighing shall
flee away."   (Isaiah vii, 21–22, and xxxv,
8–10).

With this compare the Rig Veda :—

"Do not slay the innocent cow who
is so liberal in giving her milk."   "Her

[P. 6 (cont.)]

butter (offered to the fire) is known in mysticism as the tongue of the gods and the secret of attaining immortality."

"The Sacred Fire is that which can guide us by the way of holiness (Supathā) ; it is that which can make us clean of all sins, in other words, make us fit to pass over the way of holiness (Yuyodhyasmat juhuranam enah); it is that which can, by reason of its possessing all intelligences through having connexion with the Devas (Visvāni vayunāni vidvān), do the proper guidance (so that the way-faring men, though fools, shall not err therein),; and thus we shall be all on the way to obtain joy and gladness (rāyè)."

[Texts :—" मा   गामनागामदितिं   बधिष्ट ।"
" ऋतस्य नाम गुह्यं यदस्ति जिह्वा देवानाममृतस्य नाभिः ।"
" अग्ने नय सुपथा रायेऽस्मान् विश्वानि देव वयुनानि विद्वान् ।
युयोध्यस्मज्जुह्रराणमेनो भूयिष्ठां ते नम उक्तिं विधेम ॥"—
Rig Veda Samhita, 8-101-15, 4-58-1, 1-189-1].

Thus the High Way of Isaiah (xxxv, 8) is the same as the Holy-path (Supatha) of the Rig Veda (1-189-1); and the Bible's prophecy of the protection of the cow (Isaiah vii, 21) corresponds to the Veda's prohibition of the slaughter of cows (Rig Veda, 8-101-15); the eating of butter in the Bible (Isaiah vii, 21) corresponds to the partaking of the residuary portion of the butter-libation in the Vedas (Mahabharata, Anusasanaparva, 97-7; Bhagavadgita, Ch. 3, 10 to 16, 20 to 21). Indeed, the analogy is so close that one is tempted to fancy that even the protection accorded by the Bible to the sheep (Isaiah vii, 21) corresponds to the injunctions given in the Vedic Religion to sit on fabrics made purely of sheep's wool while doing any act of devotion.

Page 7. (Chapter 1).

Note 2.   Some have supposed that the real name of the Buddha was Samantabhadra. The Amarakosha gives it as a synonym of Buddha (1-1-1-8). It is further supposed that the original image of Buddha, over which the Temple was afterwards erected, was made by some descendant of Buddha who came in succession to him to the throne of the Kingdom of Kapilavāstu. "It would appear from the tenour that Jaya Sen (Jaya Singha) and Kumara Sen (Kumara Singha), sons of Punyabhadra,

son of Samanta, erected the image as a monument of their father's holiness. Another image, according to the inscription on it, was erected by a Raja Vijayabhadra, of whom nothing more is known."
—Hamilton's Description of the Ruins of. Buddha Gaya (Transactions of the Royal Asiatic Society, London, 1830, Vol. 2). [*Cf.* Dr. Puini: Di una singolare incarnazione di Samantabhadra Bodhisattva (Rivista degli studi Orientali, Rome 6th year, 1914, pp. 989-998)].

This supposition, however, wants corroborative evidence.

Page 8.

Note 2. Hemadri, Bratakhanda, Ch. 15:—

"अनेन विधिना पूर्वं द्वादश्यौ समुपोषिता । शुद्धोदनेन बुद्धोऽभूत् खयं पुत्रो जनार्दनः ॥" Also, Bhavisya Purana, 2-83, where it is more expressly stated thus: "शुद्धोदनेन तस्याऽभूत् खयं पुत्रो जनार्दनः ।" (2-83-116). Meaning: "By virtue of Suddhaudana or the purity of his food, God Himself took birth as his son."

Page 9.

Note 1. Amarakosha, 1-1-1-10:—

"गौतमश्चार्कबन्धुश्च मायादेवीसुतश्च सः ।"

(91)

Abhidhana-chintamani, 2-149 to 151:—

"शाक्यसिंहोऽर्कबान्धवः "

Vaijayanti-kosha, 1-1-35:—

" गौतमस्त्वार्कबन्धुश्च ।"

Note 2. Rig Veda, 3-5-4:—

"The Mitra (or Sun) is a fiercely burning fire."

("मित्रोऽग्निर्भवति यत् समिद्धः ") ।

The same, 10-45-1:—

" Fire was born first as the Sun."

("दिवस्परि प्रथमं जज्ञे अग्निः") ।

Note 3. The veneration for the Aswattha or Bodhi
tree (ficus religiosa) among the Buddhists
may be traced to the ancient fire-worship
of the Hindus. The wood of this tree
was specially used for the fire-drill, and so
the tree came to be regarded as sacred
by the Hindus. This regard for the tree
was maintained by Buddha who handed it
down to his followers. See Rhys Davids,
Buddhist India, p. 231.

Page 10.

Note 1. " Ushnisha-dhārana" or wearing the helmet,
is well-known in Vedic literature, especially in the rites of the Agnistoma Yajna.

Note 2. Chaitya (Lexicon) :—" चैत्यमाज्याधिवासनम् " इति वैजयन्ती, Vaijayanti, 3-6-90.

In the Vaijayanti of Yādava, the word Chaitya has been taken to mean " clearing the clarified butter (Ghrita)." (Oppert's Edn., p. 90 and p. 497). This has direct reference to the worship of the sacred fire with butter libation. *Cf.* Panini, Astadhyayi, 3-1-132 :—

" चित्याग्निचित्ये च ", from which चैत्य ।

Cf. Mugdhabodha, Bohtlingk's Edn., St. Petersburg, 26-11.

Page 11.

Note 2. The Buddhist Suttas (Rhys Davids) :—

"In great numbers, Ananda, are the gods of the ten world-systems assembled together to behold the Tathagata. For twelve leagues, Ananda, around the Sāla Grove of the Mallas, the Upavattan of Kusinārā, there is no spot in size even as the pricking of the point of the tip of a hair which is not pervaded by powerful spirits." And again : "There are spirits, Ananda, in the sky." "There are spirits, Ananda, on the earth." (Mahaparinirvana Sutra, pp. 88–89). In the Dharma-chakra-pravartana Sutra, several heavens and grades of gods are also spoken of (P. 154 of the Buddhist Suttas).

Note 3.   The Vedas require continuous libations of Ghrita to the fire; the Tantras fix the libations to one-tenth of the number of incantations.   Both the Vedas and Tantras are for the invocation of the Devas.

Page 12.

Note 2.   Lalita Vistara, Ch. 3, line 146 ff. (Lefmann):—

“ बोधिसत्त्वः कुलविलोकितं विलोकयति स्म । न बोधि-सत्त्वा हीनकुलेषूपपद्यन्ते । अथ तर्हि कुलद्वये एवोपपद्यन्ते । ब्राह्मणकुले क्षत्रियकुले च । ”

Note 3.   Satasahasrika-Prajnāpāramitā :—

“ एवं दानं दत्त्वा क्षत्रियमहाशालकुलेषूपपद्यते । एवं दानं दत्त्वा ब्राह्मणमहाशालकुलेषूपपद्यते । ”—
(quoted by Khunnilal Sastri in his Buddhāstikatā-Vichāra).   (This portion of the Satasahasrika has not yet appeared in print).

Page 13.

Note 1.   Satasahasrika-Prajnāpāramitā,   Ch.   10, p. 1460:—

“ न जातु नीचकुलेषूपपद्यते । इदं बोधिसत्त्वस्य महासत्त्वस्य मानस्तम्भनिर्घातनपरिकर्म्म । ”

The same, Ch. 10, p. 1471:—

“ बोधिसत्त्वो महासत्त्वो महाकुलेषु प्रत्याजायते । ... क्षत्रियमहाशालकुलेषु   वा   ब्राह्मणमहाशालकुलेषु   वा

[P. 13 (cont.)]

प्रत्याजायते । यतो गोचात् पौर्वका बोधिसत्त्वा अभूवन् ।
तच्च गोचे प्रत्याजायते । ”

Note 2.   Ramayana, Balakanda, 14-12 :—

“ ब्राह्मणा भुञ्जते नित्यं नाथवन्तश्च भुञ्जते ।
तापसा भुञ्जते चापि श्रमणाश्चैव भुञ्जते ॥ ”

Page 18.

Note 1.   Lalita Vistara, Ch. 25 (towards the end) ;
cf. the Variants in Lefmann :—

“ क्व भगवान्धर्मचक्रां प्रवर्त्तयिष्यसीति...वाराणस्याम्ऋषि-
पतने म्टगदावे । ”

“ पौराण ऋषीणामिहालयवरा वाराणसी नाम वरा ।
देवनागाभिष्टुतो मच्छीतलो धर्माभिनिम्नः सदा ॥ ”

Page 19.

Note 1.   Vedic Text (well-known):—

“ मा हिंस्यात् सर्वा भूतानि । ”—

(quoted in Sridhara's commentary on the
Bhagavadgita, 18-3).

“ अहिंसा   परमो   धर्म्मः ”—Mahabharata :
Adiparva, 11-13 ; Anusasanaparva, 115-1,
115-25, 116-38 ; Aswamedhaparva, 43-21.

Note 2.   The Vedic Text :—

“ सेतूंस्तर दुस्तरान् । अक्रोधेन क्रोधम् । ”
(Sama Veda, 1-6-1-9).

[P. 19 (cont.)]

The Pali Text :—

"अक्कोधेन जिने कोधं ।"

(Dhammapada, 17-3).

[Sans.—अक्रोधेन जयेत् क्रोधम् ।]

Again :—

"नहि वेरेण वेराणि सम्मन्तीध कुदाचनं ।

अवेरेण च सम्मन्ति एस धम्मो सनातनो ॥"

(Dhammapada, 1-5).

[Sans.—न हि वैरेण वैराणि शाम्यन्तीह कदाचन ।

अवैरेण च शाम्यन्ति एष धर्मः सनातनः ॥]

Note 3. Buddhist Suttas, p. 91 :—

"Don't speak to women. If they speak to you, keep wide awake."

It may be remarked here that the high tone of morality preached by Buddha led to changes in the Architecture of the time. In those days there was a current belief that the pure-minded god of thunder detested to approach obscene things and therefore the most objectionable images were put on all sides of high temples to prevent lightning fall. This was a device to serve for the lightning-conductor which was as yet unknown. Buddhism substituted Vajrāsana, a large magic disc of stone intended for the thunder to alight upon.

[P. 19 (cont.)]

Note 4. " Buddhism, like Christianity, makes much of the next world. Its rapid acceptance by Asiatic peoples was in large measure due to its spirituality, to its emphasis on a future life, and to its denial of final significance in the everyday life one lives. The true character of the Buddhism of a country is, therefore, illustrated in its dealings with those who die." (Saunders: Buddhism and Buddhists in Southern Asia, p. 44).

" The belief that after death the departed spirits roam about enjoying the fruits of their good and bad deeds here upon earth, is one of the central ideas of the Buddhist faith, and a treatise dealing with spirits and the spirit-world, Petavatthu, is included in the Pāli sacred canon." (Law: Buddhist Conception of Spirits, p. 1).

This Buddhist belief in the survival of the soul is purely Vedic in its origin. " The belief in the existence of departed ancestors, and the presentation of offerings to them have always formed a part of Hindu domestic religion. To gratify this persistent belief, Buddhism recognised

(97)

the world of petas, i.e. ghosts or spirits."
(Sir Charles Eliot : Hinduism and Buddhism, Vol. 1, p. 338).

Page 20.

Note 1.   Buddha-charita of Aswaghosha, 12-102 ff :—

"स्वस्थप्रसन्नमनसः समाधिरुपपद्यते ।
समाधियुक्तचित्तस्य ध्यानयोगः प्रवर्त्तते ॥
ध्यानप्रवर्त्तनाद्धर्मां प्राप्यन्ते यैरवाप्यते ।
दुर्लभं ग्रान्तमजरं परं तदमृतं पदम् ॥"

Purport :—When the mind has come
to rest, then, and only then, does a man
discover the path to immortality through
yoga (dhyāna).

Note 2.   Jataka-sasthi Puja :—

"ध्यानासीनो महायोगी दौर्घायुसुखड्मुखितः ।"

Vayu Purana, 18-28 :—

"बुद्धरूपं समास्थाय योगमार्गे व्यवस्थितः ।"

Note 3.   Sankaracharya's Dasāvatāra Stotra, verse
9, line 2 :—

"कलौ योगिनां चक्रवर्त्तौ ।"

Note 5.   Bhagavadgita, 4-5 :—

"बहूनि मे व्यतीतानि जन्मानि तव चार्जुन ।
तान्यहं वेद सर्वाणि न त्वं वेत्थ परन्तप ॥"

Several passages attest to Buddha's acquirement of an extraordinary degree of concentration. A loud thunder falling close to him would not be noticed by him. Overcome with bodily sufferings he would plunge himself into such deep meditation that they could not make themselves felt by him. (Mahaparinirvana Sutra, Ch. 4, § 41 and Ch. 2, § 32).

Page 21.

Note 2.　Amarakosha, 1-1-1-9 :—

"सर्वज्ञः सुगतो बुद्ध * * अद्वयवादी विनायकः ।"

It should be noted that the Amarakosha is regarded as a Buddhist work, the author having been a worshipper of the Buddha.

Vaijayanti, 1-1-34 :—

"शाक्यो मुनिरद्वयवाद्यपि ।"

Halayudha, 1-85 :—

"* * बुद्धः शाक्यस्तथागतः सुगतः । मारजिदद्वयवादी समन्तभद्रः ।"

Note 3.　Taittiriya Upanishad, 2-1 :—

"सत्यं ज्ञानमनन्तं ब्रह्म ।"

Note 4.   The Astasahasrika begins thus :—

"ॐ नमो भगवत्यै आर्य्यप्रज्ञापारमितायै ।"

"निर्विकल्पे नमस्तुभ्यं प्रज्ञापारमितेऽमिते ॥"

"बड्रूपा त्वमेवैका नानानामभिरौड्यसे ।"

The last (or verse 9) is the doctrine of the Upanishads as to how the One becomes the Many by assuming various forms and names through Māyā (or dream-like delusion). *Cf.* "Every Buddha assembling his disciples instructs them how from unity thou (Prajnā) becomest multiformed and many-named." (Astasahasrika, quoted by Hodgson, p. 86 of his Essays).

Page 22.

Note 1.   The Jnāna Sankalini Tantra, verse 54 :—

"न ध्यानं ध्यानमित्याङ्कध्यानं शून्यगतं मनः ।"

Purport :—That is the true meditation in which the mind penetrates into the nothingness (Sunya, Maya) of things.

Note 2.   If the term Nirvana means extinction, it must be taken to mean the extinction of desires, and never the extinction of the soul (see the Yoga Vasistha, Nirvāna-prakarana). "One of the meanings attached to the Sanskrit word Nirvana is to extinguish ; therefore many learned writers have advanced the theory that

[P. 22 (cont.)]

to enter into Nirvana must mean to be extinguished and absorbed into space. But that can never be the right meaning of it according to Buddha's own teaching. 'Buddha was once asked by a man: What is Nirvana?—and Buddha answered him saying: Nirvana is the destroying of all desires.'" (From the Kanjur,—or Bkah-Hgyur,—translated by Rev. Mr. Webber and quoted by Lord Dunmore in "The Pamirs," Vol. I, pp. 122–124).

Those who wish to derive the meaning of Nirvana from the Buddha's Fire-sermon (Mahavarga, 1-21), should remember that the sermon was not original, but based upon older teachings and must therefore be interpreted in the previously accepted way. *Cf.* Yoga Vasistha: "To him whose soul is cool, the world is cool; to him whose soul is set on fire by secret desires, the world is on fire"—

"अन्तःशीतलतायां तु लब्धायां शीतलं जगत् ।

अन्तस्तृष्णोपतप्तानां दावदाहमयं जगत् ॥"—

(quoted in the Jivanmukti-viveka, Ch. 4, by Vidyaranya Swamin).

"Nirvana means nothing but a condition of perfect freedom from desire."

[P. 22 (cont.)]

" As every man through ignorance creates his own world, his own sorrow, so also every man brings to pass through knowledge his own world-cessation, his own ending of sorrow, his own Nirvana." (Paul Dahlke: "Buddhist Essays," translated by Silacara, p. 85 and p. 88). " Nirvana implies 'what is no more agitated,' 'what is in a perfect calm.' " (See Fytche: "Burma," Vol. 2, p. 173, foot-note). This state has been compared to a steady, unflickering light. The soul which was being driven from birth to rebirth owing to its being swayed by desires, now stands calm and self-possessed, being at last freed from all desires.

In the Iti-vuttaka, Buddha says: "Those who are good-minded, prudent and contemplative, who rightly discern the Law, nor look upon lusts, these are not destined to decrease even in the presence of Nirvana" (quoted by Nixon in his " Knowledge of the Buddha ").

" To Buddha himself and to his immediate disciples, it is now nearly certain that Nirvana meant, not the cessation of being, but its perfection." (Smith, Mohammed and Mohammedanism, p. 4, foot-note, Revised Edition). The Buddha himself has said : " Certainly, brothers, I teach Annihilation (Nirvana)—the Annihilation, namely, of Greed, Anger, of Delusion, of of the manifold evil, unwholesome conditions of the mind." (Majjhima Nikaya and Anguttara Nikaya, II and III).

There is, therefore, no difference between Buddha and the Hindus in the understanding of Nirvana.

Page 23.

Note 1.   Dhammapada, 11-9 (Pali Text) :—

" गहकारक दिट्ठोसि पुन गेहं न काहासि ।
सव्वा ते फासुका अगगा गहकूटं विसंखतं ।
विसङ्खारगतं चित्तं तण्हानं खयमज्जगा ॥ "

[Sans.—गृहकारक दृष्टोऽसि पुनः गेहं न कर्त्तासि ।
सर्वास्ति पार्श्वका भग्मा गृहकूटं विसंस्कृतम् ।   विसंस्कारगतं
चित्तं ट्याानां व्हयमध्यगात् ॥]

Purport :—The soul is the creator of the body. (The example of dream may make it intelligible. In dream the real body lies flat, while another and a similar body starts up in the dream and frets about in the dream-land. This dream-body is admittedly a creation of the soul, being nothing more than an internal thing

[P. 23 (cont.)]

projected as something external.   In like manner, when true awakening takes place in man, he cognizes the real body also as creation of the soul).   When perfect realisation of this fact is attained by man, he is freed from all re-births in mortal shapes.   The world being thus known to be a delusion, man reaches the state of perfect calm and desirelessness, becomes one with Brahma, the universal soul.

This is a purely Vedic teaching which the Buddha rehearses as his own creed. Elsewhere, in the Iti-vuttaka, the Buddha says : "When he (the perfect bhik·shu) hath crossed over and gone to the other shore he standeth upon the dry land of Brahma." [Quoted by Nixon in his "Knowledge of the Buddha," Maha-bodhi Journal, Vol. 31, p. 340.]

Note 3.   Taittiriya Upanishad, 2-1 :—

"ॐ ब्रह्मविदाप्नोति परम् ।"

Swetaswatara Upanishad, 6-15 :—

"तमेव विदिल्वाऽतिमृत्युमेति नान्यः पन्था विद्यतेऽयनाय ।"

The Hatha-yoga-pradipika, 4-35, 36, 37 :—

"एकैव श्राम्भवीमुद्रा गुप्ता कुलवधूरिव ।"

[P. 23 (cont.)]

" अन्तर्लच्यं बहिर्दृष्टिः " * * " सा लब्धा प्रसादाद्गुरोः । "

(The commentator Swatmārāma Swamin says that by this process is held up to the vision of man an image of Shambhu— the Ancient of Days of the Bible—whence it has been named the Shāmbhavi Mudrā). The Gheranda Samhita, Ch. 3, § 59-62 :—

" नेत्राञ्जनं समालोक्य आत्मारामं निरीक्ष्येत् ।

सा भवेच्छाम्भवीमुद्रा सर्वतन्त्रेषु गोपिता ॥

स एव आदिनाथश्च स च नारायणः स्वयम् ।

स च ब्रह्मा सृष्टिकारी यो मुद्रां वेत्ति शाम्भवीम् ॥

सत्यं सत्यं पुनः सत्यं सत्यमुक्तं महेश्वरः ।

शाम्भवीं यो विजानीयात् स च ब्रह्म न चान्यथा ॥ "

English Translation :—Fixing the eyes on the space between the two brows, behold the vision of the Ancient of Days. This is the Shāmbhavi Mudra, the secret of Siva, kept concealed in the Books. He who has once experienced this phenomenon, discovers himself to be the creator, the preserver and the destroyer of the Universe. Siva has sworn it thrice that he who has experienced this Shāmbhavi Mudra in himself is the Supreme Soul and not otherwise. With this may be compared the Vedic Text quoted below in Note 2 to p. 63, viz., Satapatha

Brahmana, 14-7-2-17, or Brihadaranyaka Upanishad, 4-4-13. (All this means only to say that this is his last birth, and that at his death he shall lapse into the Original Cause. This "yoga" should not be tried without proper guidance, as there is considerable risk of losing the sight by the strain on the eyes involved in it).

For the "stigmata" of St. Francis of Assisi and a picture of his vision of Jesus, see Bettany's World's Religions. It may be noticed here that the usual attitude of Jesus himself in his devotions, as exhibited in pictures, answers exactly to the Shāmbhavi Mudra of the yogins.

Page 24.

Note 1. The Isāvāsya Upanishad, 11 :—

"विद्यां चाविद्यां च यस्तद्वेदोभयं सह ।

अविद्यया मृत्युं तीर्त्वा विद्ययाऽमृतमश्नुते ॥"

Purport :—He who practises both action and knowledge, first elevates himself above the mortal sphere through action, and then by virtue of his knowledge sticks to the immortal sphere and there makes further progress towards perfection. (The action is the Vedic Agnihotra, as pointed out by Sankaracharya himself in his commentary to this Upanishad ; the knowledge is that of the Spirit : the suffix twā in tirtwā means succession, not simultaniety,—first the one and next the other).

Cf. "Excellent is Thorah study together with work ; and all Thorah without work must fail at length." (Pirque Aboth, 2-2)

Note 3. Rig Veda, 10-129-4 :—

"कामस्तदग्रे ममवर्त्तेताधिमनसो   रेतः   प्रथमं यदासीत् ।"

Page 25. (Chapter II).

Note 2. **Original Texts for Buddha being an Avatara of the Hindus.**

बुद्धस्याऽवतारऽविधानम ।

Matsya Purana, 47-247 :—

"कत्तं धर्म्मव्यवस्थानमसुराणां प्रगाप्रनम् ।
बुद्धो नवसको जज्ञे तपसा पुष्करेच्चगः ॥ "

Kalki Purana, 2-3-26 :—

" बुद्धावतारस्त्वमसि । "

Vayu Purana, Ekalinga Mahatmya, 12-43, 44 :—

"मत्स्यः कूर्म्मो वराहश्च नारसिंहोऽथ वामनः ।
रामो रामश्च कृषाश्च बुद्धः कल्की च ते दश ॥

[P. 25 (cont.)]

भूमेर्भारावतारगय वासुदेवो जगत्प्रभुः।
अवतारैर्दृढव्रतैरवतीर्णो मह्रीतले ॥ ”

The same, 14-39 :—

“ कृतादिषु त्रिषु हरिरवतीर्य मुञ्जर्मंछीम् ।
पाति रूपैर्नृसिंहाद्यैर्बुद्धः सोऽद्य कलौ स्थितः ॥ ”

Garuda Purana, 86-10 :—

“ धर्मसंग्रहणार्थाय अधर्मादिविनष्टये ।
दैत्यराक्षसनाशार्थं मत्स्यः पूर्वं यथाऽभवत् ॥
कूर्म्मो वराहो नृहरिर्वामनो राम उज्जितः ।
यथा दाशरथी रामः कृष्णो बुद्धोऽथ कल्क्यपि ॥ ”

Baraha Purana, 4-3 :—

“ मत्स्यः कूर्म्मो वराहश्च नरसिंहोऽथ वामनः ।
रामो रामश्च कृष्णश्च बुद्धः कल्की च ते दश ॥
इत्येताः कथितास्तस्य मूर्त्तयो भूतधारिणि ।
दर्शनं प्राप्तमिच्छूनां सोपानानि च प्रोभने ॥ ”

The same, 113-27 :—

“ मत्स्यः कूर्म्मो वराहश्च नारसिंहोऽथ वामनः ।
रामो रामश्च कृष्णश्च बुद्धः कल्की महात्मवान् ॥ ”

Nrisingha Purana, 36-29 :—

“ कलौ पापे यथा बुद्धो भवेन्नारायणः प्रभुः । ”

[Other references :—Agni Purana, 16-1 ;
Bhagavata Purana, 6-8-17 ; Brihannāradiya Purana, 2-39 ; Garuda Purana,
1-149-39, 1-202-11 ; Garga Samhita, Aswa-
medha Khanda, 59-119, and Balabhadra
Khanda, 12-25 ; Vayu Purana, 15-51, 9-19
(Ekalinga Mahatmya) ; Sankara Vijaya,

12-8 ; Gita Govinda (in the hymn to the Avataras) ; Apāmārjana Stotra (the passage beginning with "मत्स्यः कूर्मो वराहश्च ") ; Nārada Pancha-ratra (the passage beginning with "बुद्धो ध्यानजिताप्रेषदेव ") ; Subhāsita Ratnabhāndāgāram (the passage beginning with "यस्यालीयत प्राल्कसौन्नि जलधिः ") ; Hemadri, Brata Khanda, Ch. 15 ("शुद्धोदनेन बुद्धोऽभूत् स्वयं पुत्रो जनार्दनः ।").]

Purport :—All the texts cited above are from the authoritative Hindu Scriptures. They all declare that Buddha was the ninth incarnation of Narayana, the Supreme Spirit,—the incarnation for the Kali Age. It is hardly necessary to say that the Avatara (incarnation of God) is the highest object of worship among the Hindus, and that Buddha is that object in the present Age.

Page 26.

Note 1.   Bhagavadgita, 4-7, 8 :—

"यदा यदा हि धर्मस्य ग्लानिर्भवति भारत ।
अभ्युत्थानमधर्मस्य तदात्मानं सृजाम्यहम् ॥
परित्राणाय साधूनां विनाशाय च दुष्कृताम् ।
धर्मसंस्थापनार्थाय सम्भवामि युगे युगे ॥ "

Purport :—When bad times come, wicked men get the upper hand and pervert

[P. 26 (cont.)]

the course of morality. At such times when daring to do the evil is counted as an act of merit, then an incarnation of God appears on the earth who pulls the thread which sets in motion the wheel of righteousness again. (Dharmachakra-pravartana Sutra).

Bhagavata Purana, 1-3-28 :—

"इन्द्रारिव्याकुलं लोकं म्डयन्ति युगे युगे । "

Garuda Purana, 1-149-39 :—

"वासुदेवः पुनर्बुद्धः सम्मोहाय सुरद्विषाम् ।

देवादिरच्चणार्थाय अधर्महरणाय च ॥ "

The same, 86-10 :—

"धर्मसंरच्चणार्थाय अधर्मातिविनष्टये ।

दैत्यराच्तसनाप्राथं ... ... बुद्धोऽथकुल्क्यपि ॥ "

[Other references :—Bhagavata Purana, 6-8-17 ; Garuda Purana, 202-11. Matsya Purana, 47-247, has been quoted above.]

Purport :—The authoritative Hindu Scriptures, in the texts cited above, declare that whenever the course of righteousness was perverted by the wick-ed, Narayana, the Supreme Spirit, des-cended on the earth in the form of an Avatara (incarnation) to set it right again, and that Buddha was such an Avatara with precisely the same function.

[P. 26 (cont.)]

Note 2. Lalita Vistara, Ch. 7. In the passage beginning with "तेन च समयेन हिमवतः," there is a graphic description of Buddha's extraordinary birth, which resembles the birth of the other Avataras (p. 101 of Lefmann's Edition).

Lalita Vistatra, Ch. 15 :—

"वज्रदृढ अभेद्य नारायण आत्मभावो गुरुवीर्य्यबलोपेतः सोऽक्रमप्यः सर्वसत्त्वोत्तमः" (in the paragraph beginning with "चत्वारस्थ महाराजानो अडक्रवतौ"—p. 202 of Lefmann's Edition).

Yoga Vasistha, Vairagya Prakarana. 26-39 :—

"परोपकाग्रकारिग्या परार्त्तिपरितप्तया ।
बुद्ध एव सुखी मन्ये स्वात्मप्रीतलया धिया ॥ "

[Commentary :—"बुद्धः प्रबुद्धतत्त्वपुरुषः ।"— भिच्छ्कतटीका ॥]

Mahabharata, Santiparva, 285-32 :—

"एतद्बुद्धा भवेद्बुद्धः किमन्यद्बुद्धलच्छणम् ।"

Mahaparinirvāna Sutra, Ch. 5 :—

"Out of reverence for the successor of the Buddhas of old." (Rhys Davids Translation of the Buddhist Suttas, p. 86)

Lalita Vistara, Ch. 12 (p. 156 of Lefmann's Edition) :—

"एष धरणिमण्डले पूर्वबुद्धासनस्थः * * * प्राप्यते बोधिमग्राम् ।"

[P. 26 (cont.)]

Lankāvatāra Sutra :—the passage beginning with

"रावणोऽहं दशग्रीवो राक्षसेन्द्र इहागतः ।

अनुगृह्णाहि मे लङ्कां ये चास्मि पुरवासिनः ॥

पूर्वैरपि च सम्बद्धैः प्रत्यात्मगतिगोचरम् ।

शिखरे रत्नखचिते पुरमध्ये प्रकाशितम् ॥"

Mention has been made there of a Buddha as well as of Purva-Buddhas.

[The Tara Tantra also makes mention of a Buddha in the time of Vasistha.]

List of Purva-Buddhas in p. 229 of the "Useful Tables" in Vol. 2 of Prinsep's "Antiquities" :-

(1) Vipasya.

(2) Sikhi.

(3) Viswa Bhu.

(4) Karkut Chand.

(5) Kanak Muni.

(6) Kasyapa, and

(7) Sakya Sinha (the present Buddha).

Purport :—The texts and references cited above from both Hindu and Buddhist Scriptures, prove this that of the many Buddhas the one who is the chief object of worship among the Buddhists is the Avatara of the Hindus and, consequently, the chief object of worship among the latter also.

Page 27.

Note 1. According to some, Buddha, born at Kapila-vāstu, the abode of Kapila, was the real successor of Kapila, and his system was only the logical outcome of the system of Kapila, called the Sānkhya Philosophy. (*Cf.* Rajendralala Mitra, in his Preface to the " Yoga Aphorisms of Patanjali," p. v. *Cf.* also Dr. Hermann Jacobi: Buddhistischen Philosophie zu Shānkhya-Yoga und die Bedeutung der Nidanas, Leipsic ; and Colebrooke's Essays, I, p. 93).

Note 2. **Original Texts for Buddha's Murtipuja or idolisation.**

बुद्धस्य मूर्त्तिपूजाविधानम् ।

Linga Purana, 2-48-28 to 33 :—

" मत्स्यः कूर्मोऽथ वाराहो नारसिंहोऽथ वामनः ।

रामो रामश्च कृष्णश्च बुद्धः कल्की तथैव च ।

तेषामपि च गायत्रीं ज्ञात्वा स्थाप्य च पूजयेत् ॥ "

Agni Purana, 49-8 :—

" शान्तात्मा लम्बकर्णश्च गौराङ्गश्चाम्बराटतः ।

ऊर्ध्वपद्मस्थितो बुद्धो वरदाभयदायकः ॥ "

Bhavisya Purana, 2-73 :—

" सुवर्णमयीं भगवतः श्रीबुद्धदेवस्य प्रतिमां स्थापयित्वा-

ऽर्चयित्वा च ब्राह्मणाय दद्यात् । "

[P. 27 (cont.)]

Hemadri, Chaturvarga Chintamani, Brata-Khanda, Ch. 1 (p. 119 of Asiatic Society's Edition) :—

"काषायवस्त्रसम्बीतः स्कन्धे संसक्तचीबरः ।

पद्मासनस्थो द्विभुजो ध्यायौ बुद्धः प्रकीर्त्तितः ॥"

The same, Ch. 15 (p. 1038 of Asiatic Society's Edition) :—

"बुद्धस्तु द्विभुजः कार्यो ध्यानस्तिमितलोचनः ।"

[Other references :—Bhavisya Purana, 2-73 (the passage beginning with "दश्रावतारा- नभ्यर्चत् पुष्पधूपविलेपनैः"); Hemadri, Brata-Khanda, Ch. 15 ("स्थापयेत्तत्र सौवर्णं बुद्धं कृत्वा विचक्षणः," in the passage beginning with "एवमेव श्रावणे मासि ।").]

Purport :—The above are all texts from the Hindu Scriptures giving directions to Hindus to make idols of Buddha by which to promulgate his worship. It is worth remarking that all the images of Buddha which are worshipped by the Buddhists also, answer exactly to these directions given by the Hindu Scriptures.

Note 3. Suta Samhita, 4-3-21 :—

"बुद्धार्हतादिमार्गस्थे देवताप्रतिमास च ।

देवताबुद्धिमाचं यत्स्योऽपि यज्ञः प्रकीर्त्तितः ॥"

[P. 27 (cont.)]

Suta Gita, 8-35 :—

"तंत्रोक्तेन प्रकारेण देवता या प्रतिष्ठिता ।

साऽपि वन्द्या सुसेव्या च पूजनीया च वैदिकैः ॥"

Purport :—The firm conviction in the existence of gods as beings superior to man, whether it take the form of idol-worship or not, is also classed as Yajña or the method of worship authorised by the Vedas. The idols which have been established by the rules of the Tantras, are all to be worshipped also by the followers of the Vedas.

Note 4. **Original Text for Symbol-worship of Buddha—Buddha's Sālagrāma.**

बुद्धस्य ग्रालग्रामविधानम् ।

Brahmanda Purana :—

"अयागच्छद्ररसंयुक्तं चक्रचह्नीनं यथा भवेत् ।

निविडो बुद्धसंज्ञः स्याद्दराति परमं पदम् ॥"

Purport :—Round stone images, called Salagramas, have diverse sorts of marks and holes. Each stone, according to its special features, is known as a particular form of Vishnu, such as Sridhara, Lakshmi-Narayana, Padmanāva, Raghunātha, Rana-raghu, etc. A Sālagrama that is endued with a small hole and divested of

(115)

circular marks, and is close-grained, is
known as the symbol of Buddha. It
being worshipped, the Buddha himself is
worshipped, and the same result is attained in both cases. All this is meant for
the Hindus by the Hindu Scriptures
themselves.

[N.B. The above text is to be found
in the Pranatoshini Tantra, in the fourth
chapter of the fifth Kanda, where it is
cited as a quotation from the Brahmanda
Purana]

Page 28.

Note 1. **Original Text for wearing the Tilaka or mark
on the forehead to indicate the Buddha's
devotee among the Hindus.**

बुद्धस्य पुण्ड्रधारणविधानम् ।

Suta Samhita, Suta Gita, 8-34 :—

"अश्वत्थपत्रसदृशं हरिचन्दनेन

मध्ये ललाटमतिशोभनमादरेण ।

बुद्धागमे मुनिवरा यदि संस्कृतस्थे-

न्मुद्रारिणा सततमेव तु धारयेच्च ॥ "

Purport :—If Hindu ascetics (Munis)
are initiated (sanskrita) into the rites of
Buddha's worship (Buddhāgama), they
should, to indicate their sect, always
wear a mark on the forehead resembling

[P. 28 (cont.)]

the leaf of the Pippala or Bodhi tree (Aswattha-patra), and made with yellow sandal-wood paste (Harichandana).

This and the preceding texts are intended for Hindu idolators only, who alone are used to such practices. Various forms of Tilaka are used to indicate the various sects of worshippers.

In connection with what follows, it should be noticed that not only the Java images, but Tibetan, Burmese, Japanese, Ceylonese and Chinese images also, show the Tilaka on the forehead of Buddha. (See Karl With : Java, Plates 10 to 12 ; H. G. Wells : A Short History of the World, pp. 151 and 152 ; Anesaki : Buddhist Art, Plate 12 ; Woodward : Buddhist Ceylon, Frontispiece ; Ashton : Chinese Sculpture, Plate 53, Buddha in Maitreya's Paradise).

The sacred thread depicted on the Java images (Karl With : Plates 8 to 11) is corroborated by Saubhagya Bijaya, the Jaina authority, who says that the Janoi (Yajñopavita or Brahmanical sacred thread) is the distinguishing feature of Buddha's images. (See below, Notes to p. 33).

(117)

[P. 28 (cont.)]

Note 2. **Original Texts for Buddha's Pratah-smara-nam or early morning salutation.**

बुद्धस्य प्रातःस्मरणविधानम् ।

Garuda Purana, 2-31-35 :—

"मत्स्यं कूर्मं च वराहं नारसिंहं च वामनम् ।

रामं रामश्च कृष्णश्च बुद्धश्चैव सकल्किनम् ।

एतानि दशनामानि स्मर्त्तव्यानि सदा बुधैः ॥"

Bhagavata Purana, 1-3-29 :—

"जन्म गुह्यं भगवतो य एतत् प्रयतो नरः ।

सायं प्रातर्गृणन् भक्त्या दुःखग्रामादिमुच्यते ॥"

Purport :—The Hindu Scriptures enjoin all the Hindus regularly to recollect the name and incarnation of Buddha as the first thing on waking up ; and a great merit is awarded for this act.

Note 3. **Original Texts for Buddha's Meditation.**

बुद्धस्य ध्यानविधानम् ।

Agni Purana, 49-8 :—

"प्रशान्तात्मा लम्बकर्णश्च गौराङ्गश्चाम्बरावृतः ।

ऊर्ध्वपद्मस्थितो बुद्धो वरदाभयदायकः ॥"

Meru Tantra, Ch. 36 (Avatara Prakarana) :—

"पद्मे पद्मासनस्थं तमूर्ध्वान्यस्तकरद्वयम् ।

गौरं मुदितसर्वाङ्गं ध्यानस्तिमितलोचनम् ॥

पुस्तकासक्तहस्तैश्च नानाभिष्टैश्च शोभितम् ।

इन्द्रादिलोकपालैश्च नतं त्वेनाम्बरावृतम् ॥"

(118)

Sankaracharya (Hymn to the Ten Avataras) :—

" धराबद्धपद्मासनस्याङ्गयष्टि-

निर्यद्भ्यानिलं न्यस्तनासाग्रदृष्टिः

य आस्ते कलौ योगिनां चक्रवर्त्ती

स बुद्धः प्रबुद्धोऽस्तु मच्चित्तवर्त्ती ।"

Purport :—Not only the Hindu Scriptures, but even Sankaracharya, who is supposed by some to have been an opponent of Buddhism, gives directions to the Hindus as to how to meditate on the Buddha.

Page 29

Note 1. **Original Texts for Buddha's Bratapuja or Ritualistic Worship.**

बुद्धस्य व्रतपूजाविधानम

Agni Purana, 16-1 :—

" वच्ये बुद्धावतारश्च पठतः प्रयतवतोऽर्घदम् ।"

Garuda Purana, 1-2-32 :—

" संपूज्यश्च व्रतादिना ।"

The same, 1-149-39 :—

" वासुदेवः पुनर्बुद्धः * * * श्रुत्वा खगं व्रजेन्नरः ।"

Baraha Purana, 211-65 to 66 :—

" पूजयेत् कमलैर्देवि मद्भक्तः संयतेन्द्रियः ।

मत्स्यं कूर्मं वराहञ्च नरसिंहं च वामनम् ॥

रामं रामञ्च कृष्णां च बुद्धं चैव च कल्किनम् ।

एवं दशावतारांश्च पूजयेद्भक्तिसंयुतः ॥"

[P. 29 (cont.)]

The same, 48-22 :—

"रूपकामो यजेद्बुद्धं प्रतुघातोय कल्किनम् ।"

The same, 49 (the whole chapter, beginning with the words "In the month of Sravana") :—

"श्रावणे मासि शुक्लायामित्यारभ्य अध्यायसमाप्तिपर्य्यन्तं बुद्धदादशीव्रतकथा ।"

Bhavisya Purana, 2-73 :—

"एवं श्रावणशुक्लादादश्यां बुद्धाय नमः पादयाः । श्रीधराय नमः कट्याम् । पद्मोद्भवाय नमः उदरे । सम्बत्सराय नमः उरसि । सुग्रीवाय नमः कण्ठे । विश्वबाहवे नमः भुजयोः । प्राज्ञाय नमः प्राङ्ख् । चक्राय नमः चक्र ॥ एभिर्मन्त्रैः सम्पूज्य कलशे सुवर्णमयीं भगवतः श्रीबुद्धदेवस्य प्रतिमां स्थापयित्वा अर्चयित्वा च ब्राह्मणाय दद्यात् ।"

The same (Bhavisya Purana, 2-73) :—

"दशावतारानभ्यर्चयेत् पुण्यधूपविलेपनैः ।

*   *   *

मत्स्यं कूर्मं वराहं च नारसिंहं त्रिविक्रमम् ।
रामं रामं च कृष्णं च बुद्धं च कल्किनं तथा ॥

*   *   *

अत्र हैमीर्महार्हाश्च दशमूर्त्तौः सुलक्षणाः ।
गन्धपुष्पैश्च नैवेद्यैरर्चयेद्विधिपूर्वकम् ॥"

Hemadri, Chaturvarga Chintāmani, Brata-Khanda, Ch. 15 :—

"एवमभ्यर्च्य मेधावी तस्याग्रे पूर्ववद्घटम् ।
स्थापयेत्तच्च सौवर्णं बुद्धं कृत्वा विचक्षणः ।
तमप्येवं तु सम्पूज्य ब्राह्मणाय निवेदयेत् ॥"

(120)

[P. 29 (cont.)]

Nirnaya Sindhu, Ch. 2 :—

"पौषशुक्लस्य सप्तम्यां कुर्य्याद्बुद्धस्य पूजनम् ।"

[Other references :—Bratarāja (in the chapter on Ananta Brata, the fifth section on Āvarana Puja); Pratisthā Mayukha ("बुद्धाय नमो बुद्धौ") ; and in the Jataka-Sasthi Puja ("स एतु जातकं नित्यं बुद्धरूपी जनार्दनः ।").]

Purport :—A system of ritualistic worship of Buddha, with various items for various occasions, has been ordained by the Hindu Scriptures for all Hindus, and not merely for those who have a predilection for the Buddha's worship.

Note 2. **Original Text for the Gāyatri or Vedic Formula of Buddha's worship.**

बुद्धस्य गायत्रीविधानम् ।

Linga Purana, 2-48-28 to 33 :—

"मत्स्यः कूर्म्मोऽथ वाराहो नारसिंहोऽथ वामनः ।

रामो रामश्च कृष्णश्च बुद्धः कल्की तथैव च ।

तेषामपि च गायत्रीं कृत्वा स्थाप्य च पूजयेत् ॥"

Purport :—The Hindus are directed to worship the Buddha in the same manner as they are to worship the other Avataras; *viz.*, by making an image unto him and

(121)

[P. 29 (cont.)]

framing a formula (of prayer to him) according to the rules of the Vedas.

Note 3. **Original Text for the Mantram of Buddha.**

बुद्धस्य मन्त्रविधानम् ।

Meru Tantra, Avatara Prakarana, Ch. 36 :—

"एवं ध्यात्वा यजेत् पद्मे द्वात्रिंशद्दलसम्मिते ।

कर्णिकायां षडङ्कानि दले शिष्यान् यजेत् क्रमात् ॥

वर्णलक्षं जपेन्मन्त्रं होमयेच्च घृतौदनम् ।

तुलसीमिश्रतोयैश्च भगवन्तं प्रतर्पयेत् ॥

एवं बुद्धं समाराध्य भुक्तिं मुक्तिं प्रयान्ति ते ॥"

[Another reference:—Bhavisya Purana, 2-73, twice in the same chapter,—quoted above.]

Purport :—The real worship of Buddha, by which one can attain to Nirvana with him, is here stated. One should repeat his incantation ("नमो भगवते बुद्धाय") nine hundred thousand times (or rather four times of that) ; give unto the sacred fire, as offering to him, rice boiled with Ghrita or melted butter, (counting by handfuls—the total count of the handfuls to be one-tenth of the number of incantations) ; and, finally, pour a libation to him of water mixed with Tulasi-leaves (the Ocimum Sanctum or Basil-leaves).

[P. 29 (cont.)]

The Meru Tantra is a Hindu work of ritualistic authority. It speaks for the Hindus and Buddhists alike. According to some, boiled rice is not to be offered by any Brahmana devotee of the Buddha : it is meant for the lower castes only. But the Mantram, with libation of Ghrita to the Sacred Fire, is open to all.

It may be remarked here that the prohibition of "boiled-rice offering" to the higher castes has come to be mistaken for prohibition of the worship of Buddha to them. So the Buddha's worship is practically left to the lower castes and foreigners, who may be seen offering boiled rice in their acts of devotion. This accounts for the perversions in the worship of Dharma Thakur, which is in fact Buddha's worship.

Note 4. Original Texts for Buddha's Namaskara or acknowledging Buddha as an object of worship.

बुद्धस्य नमस्कारविधानम् ।

Bhāgavata Purana, 10-40-22 :—

"नमो बुद्धाय शुद्धाय दैत्यदानवमोहिने ।"

(123)

[P. 29 (cont.)]

Kurma Purana, 6-15 :—

"नमो बुद्धाय शुद्धाय नमस्ते ज्ञानरूपिणे ।"

The same, 10-48 :—

"नमो बुद्धाय शुद्धाय नमो मुक्ताय हेतवे ।

नमो नमो नमस्तुभ्यं मायिने वेधसे नमः ॥"

Vayu Purana, 30-225 :—

"नमः शुद्धाय बुद्धाय शोभनाचादताय च ।"

Baraha Purana, 55-37 :—

"नमोऽस्तु ते बुद्ध कल्किन् वरेण ।"

Padma Purana, Kriyā Khanda, 6-188 :—

"तस्मै बुद्धाय ते नमः ।"

The same, 11-94 :—

"नमो बुद्धाय शुद्धाय सुद्धपाय नमो नमः ।"

Padma Purana, Sristi Khanda, 73-92 :—

"नमोऽस्तु बुद्धाय च दैत्यमोहिने ।"

Garga Samhita, Viswajit Khanda, 13-49 :—

"नमो बुद्धाय शुद्धाय कल्किने चार्त्तिहारिणे ।"

Meru Tantra, Avatara Prakarana, Ch. 36 :—

"नमो भगवते बुद्ध संसारार्णवतारक ।

कलिकालादहं भीतः शरणं शरणाङ्गतः ॥"

(With this last compare the Buddhist
formula of prayer : "बुद्धं शरणं गच्छामि")

[Other references :—Mahābhārata, Santiparva, Bhisma Stavarāja ("बुद्धरूपं ममास्थाय
बज्ररूप परायणः । मोहयन् सर्वभूतानि तस्मै मोहात्मने
नमः ॥") Tantrasara, Vishnu Stotra ("तं

[P. 29 (cont.)]

मूलभूतं प्रभातोऽस्मि बुद्धम् ''); Devi Bhāgavata, 10-5-14 ; Dasāvatāra Khanda Prasasti Kāvyam (the passage beginning with " षट्चक्रे क्रमभावनापरिगतं ").

In this last-mentioned passage, there is a remarkable portion which is worth quoting :

" May the Buddha be your guide, the Buddha who is genuine in his meditation, who openeth not his eyes from sentiments of pity at seeing that the bodies which all human creatures possess contain many holes from which filthy secretions— semen and blood, stools and urine, tears and exudations—constantly ooze out.

' Having recourse to the pretext of meditation, who is that woman of whom thou art thinking ? Cast a glance at this female who is being consumed by the passion of love for thee. That thou hast compassion is false. Where is that other male who is more cruel than thou ? ' May the Buddha, who, although thus addressed repeatedly by the fairies of Cupid's train, stirreth not yet from his meditation, may that foremost of genuine personalities be your guide in life."]

Page 30.

Note 1. **Original Texts for the holiness of Buddha-Gaya and for pilgrimage thereto.**

बुद्धगयातीर्थमाहात्म्यम् ।

Brihannila Tantram, Patala 5 :

" पृष्टा तानि महाप्राज्ञे पीठस्थानानि यानि तु ।

सिद्धिप्रदानि साधनां महद्भिः सेवितानि च ॥

*　　　　*　　　　*

पाटला च महाबोधिनंगतीर्थं मदन्तिके ।

*　　　　*　　　　*

अत्रायं तद्ब्रवेत् कार्यं पितॄणां परमं शुभम् ।

अस्मिन् स्थाने जपेद्यस्तु सिद्धिर्भवति तत्क्षणात् ॥ "

Skanda Purana, Abanti Khanda, 68-30 :

" पुरुषोत्तमगिरिः श्रेष्ठो यच्च बुद्धगया स्मृता । "

The same, 70-4 :

" फल्गुश्च सरितां श्रेष्ठा तथैव फलदायिनी ।　आदिगया

बुद्धगया तथा विष्णुपदौ स्मृता ॥ "

Vayu Purana, 2-49-26 :—

" धर्मं धर्मेश्वरं नत्वा महाबोधितरुं नमेत् । "

The same, 2-49-31 (found in some Editions):—

" चलह्रदाय तृप्ताय सर्वदा स्थितिहेतवे ।

बोधिसत्त्वाय यज्ञाय व्यक्त्याय नमो नमः ॥ "

Agni Purana, 115-37 :

" महाबोधितरुन्नत्वा धर्मवान् स्वर्गलोकभाक् । "

[P. 30 (cont.)]

[Another reference :—Gaya-Prakarana, in the work of Narayana-Bhatta called the Tristhalisetu (the passage beginning with "ततो मद्दाबोधिवतरोरधः ।").]

Purport :—The Hindus are enjoined to regard the place Mahabodhi (or Buddha-Gaya), its river (the Phalgu), and its tree (the Bodhi or Mahabodhi tree), as sacred, and to make pilgrimage to adore them. Further, when they arrive there on their pilgrimage, they are first to adore Dharmeswara the Lord of Righteousness, or Buddha, and after him, the Bodhi tree. This is expressly laid down by the authority of the Hindu Scriptures themselves. (*Cf*. Vayu Purana, cited above, where the words " natwa " and " namet " indicate the order as to which to do first and which next). The term Dharmeswara as well as Dharmaraja refers to the Buddha. (See Sherring's Benares, Ch. 5, p. 86 ; and *cf* Amarakosha, 1-1-1-8).

Page 32.

Note 1.   Vayu Purana, 2-49-26 :—

"धर्म्मं धर्म्मेश्वरं नत्वा मद्दाबोधितरुं नमेत् ।"

(The text has been just explained above).

Note 2.   Lalita Vistara, Ch. 7; in the passage beginning with "तेन च समयेन हिमवतः।" (Lefmann's
Edition, p. 101, line 13) :—

"धार्मिको धर्मराजः।"

The Buddhist formula of prayer :—

"धर्म्मं शरणं गच्छामि।"

Page 33.

Note 1.   Amarakosha, 1-1-1-8 :–

"बुद्धो धर्मराजस्तथागतः।"

Vaijayantikosha, 1-1-33 :—

"बुद्धस्तु * * धर्मराजस्तथागतः।"

Note 3.   The well-known Jaina Monk Saubhagya
Bijaya who visited Buddha-Gaya about
A.D. 1600 describes the image of Buddha
in the Great Temple as something opposed
to his own faith of Jainism.   See his
Tirthamāla-Stavana, Ch. 10, verses 2 to
5 :—

"तिहांथी बोधगया कोस चणा छे रे।

प्रतिमा बोधतणो नहिं पार रे॥

जिनमुद्राथी विपरीत जाणजे रे।

कराठ जनोईनो आकार रे॥"

Purport :—The image of Buddha is distinguished from Jaina images by its
having " Janoi," the Brahmanical sacred
thread, round the neck.   Such images are
countless in number.

(128)

(This opposition of Jainism to both Hinduism and Buddhism tends to prove the identity of the two latter—the fact being strengthened by Buddha's wearing the sacred thread of the Hindus).

The original MSS. may be seen at the Museum and Library of P. C. Nahar, Zamindar, Calcutta. The book has been printed at Bhavnagar in the Prachina Tirthamala Samgraha, Part I.

Page 34.

Note 3.   Bhagavata Purana, 1-3-24, ff. :—

"ततः कलौ संप्रवृत्ते संमोहाय सुरद्विषाम् ।
बुद्धो नाम्ना जिनसुतः कीकटेषु भविष्यति ।
इन्द्रारिव्याकुलं लोकं म्रडयन्ति युगे युगे ॥
जन्म गुह्यं भगवतो य एतत्प्रयतो नरः ।
सायं प्रातर्गृणन् भक्त्या दुःखग्रामादिमुच्यते ॥ "

Page 35.

Note. 1.   Garuda Purana, 1-2-32 :—

"ततः कलेस्तु सन्ध्यायां संमोहाय सुरद्विषाम् ।
बुद्धो नाम्ना जिनसुतः कीकटेषु भविष्यति ।
तस्मात्सर्गादयो जाताः संपूज्यश्च व्रतादिना ॥ "

Note 2.   The same, 2-31-35 :—

"मत्स्यं कूर्मं च वराहं नारसिंहं च वामनम् ।
रामं रामं च कृष्णश्च बुद्धश्चैव कल्किनम् ।
एतानि दशनामानि स्मर्त्तव्यानि सदा बुधैः ॥ "

Note 3. The Medinikosha :—

"भगवान्ना जिने गौर्यां स्त्रियां पूज्ये तु वाच्यवत् ।"

Hemachandra, 2-130 :—

"दामोदरः श्रौरिसनातनौ विभुः पीताम्बरो मार्जं जिनौ कुमोदकः ।"

Halāyudha, 1-25 :—

"नारायणो जगन्नाथो वनमाली गदाधरः ।

सनातनो जिनः प्राम्भुर्विधिर्वेधा गदाग्रजः ॥"

St. Petersburg Dictionary, s.v. जिन—d) Bein, Vishnu's.

Sabdakalpadruma, s.v. जिनः—"अर्हन् । बुद्धः । विष्णुः ।"

Note 4. Jishnu : "जयनाज्जिष्णुरुच्यते ।" (Mahabharata, Udyogaparva, 70-13).

Page 36.

Note 1. The time of the Elder Buddha is placed nearly 500 years before the Second Buddha. The term Elder Buddha is a mistranslation of Purva-Buddha, which means the Preceding Buddha. There was not one Purva-Buddha, but a series of them in succession. [See Wright's Nepal, Ch. 1; Rhys Davids: Buddhist Suttas, p. 86, "Successor of the Buddhas of old."]

(130)

Patell's Chronology, p. 48 :—

Sir William Jones fixes the date of Buddha at 1027 B.C., Prof. Wilson fixes the date of a second Buddha at 638 B.C., —both concurring with Klaproth. The Buddha of 1027 B.C. is identically the same as the latter Buddha.

Page 37.

Note 1.   Lalita Vistara, Ch. 25 (Lefmann's Edition, p. 400) :—

"पूरयन्ति धर्मं मगधेषु सत्त्वाः ।"

Note 3.   Bhagavata Purana, 1-3-24 ; Garuda Purana, 1-2-32 ; the same, 1-149-39 :—

"सम्मोहाय सुरद्विषाम् ।"

Note 4.   Suta Samhita, Brahma-Gita, 4-66 to 70 :—

"तस्मादस्ति * * * आनन्दरूपः सम्पूर्णः ।

इयमेव तु तर्काणां निष्ठाकाष्ठा सुरोत्तमाः ।

बुद्धागमानां सर्वेषां तथैवार्हागमस्य च ॥"

Purport :—Theism is ultimately reached by reaction from atheism, as the logical outcome of its own critical arguments.

Page 38.

Note 1.   Vishnu Purana, 3-18-15 ff. :—

"मायामोह उवाच ।

स्वर्गार्थं यदि वाञ्छा वो निर्वाणार्थमथासुराः ।

तदलं पशुघातादिदुष्टधर्मान्निबोधत ॥

(131)

[P. 38 (cont.)]

*   *   *

जगदेतदनाधारं भ्रान्तिज्ञानार्थतत्परम् ।

रागादिदुष्टमत्यर्थं भ्राम्यते भवसङ्कटे ॥

पराशर उवाच ।

एवं बुध्यत बुध्यध्वं बुध्यतैवमितीरयन् ।

*   *   *

दैतेयान् मोहयामास मायामोहोऽतिमोहकृत् ॥ "

Note 2.   Nārada Pancha-ratra 4-3-156 ff. :—

"बुद्धो ध्यानजिताशेषदेवदेवो जगत्प्रियः ।

निरायुधो जगज्जैत्रः श्रीघनो दुष्टमोहनः ॥

दैत्यवेदबहिष्कर्त्ता वेदार्थश्रुतिगोपकः ।

प्रौढोदार्निनष्टदृष्टिः सुखदः सदसत्पतिः ।

यथायोग्याखिलरूपः सर्वशून्योऽखिलेष्टदः ॥

चतुष्कोटि एथकृतत्त्व प्रज्ञापारमितेश्वरः ।

पाषण्डश्रुतिमार्गेण पाषण्डश्रुतिगोपकः ॥ "

Note 3.   Tantrasāra, Ch. 4 (in the Vishnu Stotra,
           verse 9) :—

"पुरा सुराणामसुरान्विजेतुं सम्भावयंस्त्रीवरचिन्हदेहाम् ।

चकार यः प्रास्त्रममोघकल्पं तं मूलभूतं प्रगतोऽस्मि
           बुद्धम् ॥ "

Note 4.   Lalita Vistara, Ch. 12 (Lefmann's Edition,
           p. 156) :—

"अथ धर्मगणमण्डले पूर्वं बुद्धासनस्थः

समर्थधनुर्गृहीत्वा शून्यनैरात्मबाणैः ।

(132)

क्षोभरिपुं निश्चला दृष्टिजालञ्च भित्त्वा
त्रिववविरजमश्लोकां प्राप्यते बोधिमग्र्याम् ॥"

Note 5. Rig Veda Samhita, 10-72-2 :—

"देवानां पूर्वे युगेऽसतः सदजायत ।"

The same, 10-129-7 :—

"इयं विस्ष्ट्रिर्यत आबभूव यदि वा दधे यदि वा न ।"

Chhandogya Upanishad, 6-2-1 :—

"तद्धैक आङ्गरसदेवेदमग्र आसीदेकमेवाद्वितीयं तस्मा-
दसतः सञ्जायत ।" [On this, see Gough:
Philosophy of the Upanishads, p. 185.]

Taittiriya Upanishad, 2-7 :—

"असद्वा इदमग्र आसीत् ततो वै सदजायत ।"

Sariraka Bhasya, 2-4-1 (quotes as a Vedic
Text) :—

"तदाङ्गः किं तदसदासीदिति ऋषयो वाव तेऽग्रे-
ऽसदासीत् ।"

Purport :—Non-existent was all this in
the beginning ; from the non-existent
came out the existent. [These are Vedic
Texts having reference to Māyā or world-
delusion.]

Page 39.

Note 1. Kurma Purana, 10-48 :—

"नमो बुद्धाय शुद्धाय * * मायिने वेधसे नमः ।"

Bhagavata Purana, 10-40-22 :—

"नमो बुद्धाय शुद्धाय दैत्यदानवमोहिने ।"

(133)

Mahabharata, Bhisma Stavaraja :—

"बुद्धरूपं समास्थाय बुद्धरूपपरायणाः ।

मोहयन् सर्वभूतानि तस्मै मोहात्मने नमः ॥"

(This last is not found in all texts).

Note 2. Devi Bhagavata, Book IV (Chapters 10–13):
the passage beginning with "ततः परस्परं युद्धं
जातं परमदारुणम् ।" (Book IV, Ch. 10, verses
39 and ff.).

Matsya Purana, 24-37 to 49: the passage beginning with "अथ देवासुरं युद्धमभूदर्षं प्रतञ्चयम् ।"
(Ch. 24, verses 37 and ff., esp. verse 47).

Note 3. Siva Purana, Rudra Samhita, Kumara
Khanda, 9-18 to 25 :—

"तच्च विष्णुश्छलौ दोषौ छ्याविवेकौ विशेषतः ।

बलियेन पुरा बुद्धश्छलमाश्रित्य पापतः ॥

तेनैव यत्नतः पूर्वमसुरौ मधुकैटभौ ।

म्रिरोच्चीनौ क्षतौ धौर्य्यादिदमार्गो विवर्जितः ॥

मोहिनौरूपतोऽनेन पङ्क्तिभेदः क्षतो ह्नि वै ।

देवासुरसुधापाने वेदमार्गो विगर्हितः ॥

रामो भूत्वा हता नारी वाली विध्वंसितो ह्नि सः ।

पुनर्वश्रवणो विप्रो हतो नीतिर्हता श्रुतः ॥

पापं विना स्वकीया स्त्री त्यक्ता पापरतेन यत् ।

तच्चापि श्रुतिमार्गस्य ध्वंसितः स्वार्थहेतवे ॥

स्वजनन्याः म्रिरस्छिन्नमवतारे रसाख्यके ।

गुरुपुत्राप्रमानश्च क्षतोऽनेन दुरात्मना ॥

क्षत्रो भूत्वाऽन्या नार्यश्च दूषिताः कुलधर्मतः ।
श्रुतिमार्गं परित्यज्य खविवाह्याः कृतास्तथा ॥
पुनश्च वेदमार्गो हि निन्दितो नवमे भवे ।
स्थापितं नास्तिकमतं वेदमार्गविरोधकृत् ॥ "

Purport :—Vishnu himself and all his
incarnations practised deception and com-
mitted acts which are condemned by the
Vedas and are repugnant to morality

Note 4. Bhagavad Gita, 15-15 :—

" मत्तः स्मृतिर्ज्ञानमपोहनञ्च । "

Page 40.

Note 1. Kaushitaki Upanishad, 3-9 :—

" एष ह्येवैनं साधुकर्म्म कारयति तं यमन्वानुनेष्यष
एवैनमसाधुकर्म्म कारयति तं यमेभ्यो लोकेभ्यो नुनुत्सते : "

A better reading is given in Cowell's Edition, p. 101 :-

" एष ह्यत्र साधु कर्म कारयति तं यमेभ्यो लोंक़भ्य
उन्निनीषत एष उ एवासाधु कर्म कारयति तं यमधो
निनीषते । "

Note 2. **Original Texts for Buddha's Worship in spite
of his practising a fraud.**

बुद्धस्य कलनधर्मिल्वेऽपि पूज्यत्वविधानम्

Bhagavata Purana, 1-3-24 ff. :—

" ततः कलौ संप्रवृत्ते सम्मोहाय सुरद्विषाम् ।
बुद्धो नाम्ना जिनसुतः कीकटेषु भविष्यति ॥

[P. 40 (cont.)]

*   *   *

जन्मं गुह्यं भगवतो य एतत्प्रयतो नरः ।

सायं प्रातर्गृणन् भक्त्या दुःखग्रामादिमुच्यते ॥ ”

The same, 10-40-22 :—

“ नमो बुद्धाय शुद्धाय दैत्यदानवमोहिने । ”

Garuda Purana, 1-2-32 :—

“ ततः कलेस्तु सन्ध्यायां सम्मोहाय सुरद्विषाम् ।

बुद्धो नाम्ना जिनसुतः कीकटेषु भविष्यति ।

तस्मात् सर्गादयो जाताः संपूज्यश्च व्रतादिना ॥ ”

The same, 1-149-39 :—

“ वासुदेवः पुनर्बुद्धः सम्मोहाय सुरद्विषाम् ।

देवादिरच्छायार्थाय अधर्मचरणाय च ।

भारतांस्तावावतारांश्च श्रुत्वा स्वर्गं व्रजेन्नरः ॥ ”

Kurma Purana, 10-48 :—

“ नमो बुद्धाय शुद्धाय नमो मुक्ताय हेतवे ।

नमो नमो नमस्तुभ्यं मायिने वेधसे नमः ॥ ”

Vayu Purana, 30-225 :—

“ नमो शुद्धाय बुद्धाय क्षोभणायाच्छताय च । ”

[Other references :—Mahabharata, Santiparva, Bhisma Stavaraja ; Tantrasāra,
Vishnu Stotra ;—both quoted above.]

Purport :—The Buddha who, by beguiling the atheists from the Vedas, saved
the latter from being tampered with by
them, is to be reverentially spoken of,
heard of, saluted, and worshipped by all
the Hindus who are followers of the

Vedas. This is ordained by their own Scriptures.

Note 3. Bhagavata Purana, 6-8-17 :—

"द्वैपायनो भगवानप्रबोधाद्

बुद्धस्तु पाषण्डगणप्रमादात् ।

कल्कौ कलेः कालमलात् प्रपातु

धर्म्माबिनायोरूहतावतारः ॥"

Garuda Purana, 202-11 :—

"बुद्धः पाषण्डसङ्घातात् कल्किरवतु कल्मषात्"

[As to the meaning of पाषण्ड in the sense of those who oppose the Vedic Religion or Sanatana Dharma, see Linga Purana, 40-40 : "वर्णाश्रमाणां ये चान्ये पाषण्डाः परिपन्थिनः।"

Purport :—The Vedas are regarded as Revelations. They are, therefore, intended only for the believers—those who have faith in them. The unbelieving people, who have no faith in Revelation, would only tamper with the Vedas, or else destroy them altogether. Hence, Buddha, seeing that atheists will predominate in the Kali Yuga, came timely to devise a plan for saving the Vedas from their hands.

Page 41.

Note 2. The Sthaviras or Sthiras (i.e., the Elders) were called the Theras in Pali, and their

successors or Sthiraputras, the Thera-
puttas in Pali (i.e. sons of Theras). They
were the custodians of drugs, and the
healing art has derived its name Thera-
peutics from them.

Page 42.

Note 1. See Vincent Smith : The Oxford History
of India, Book I, Chap. 3, p. 55, Article
"No Buddhist Period."

Page 43.

Note 1. Lalita Vistara, Ch. 25 (Lefmann's Edition,
p. 400, line 19) :—

"पठन्वन्ति धर्मं मगधेषु सत्त्वाः ।"

Mahabharata, Bhismaparva, 11-36 :—

"मंगाश्च मप्रकाश्चैव मानसा मन्दगास्तथा ।
मंगा ब्राह्मणभूयिष्ठाः खकर्मनिरता ङ्ख ॥"

Vishnu Purana, 2-4-69 :—

"मगाश्च मागधाश्चैव मानसा मन्दगास्तथा ।
मगा ब्राह्मणभूयिष्ठा मागधाः क्षत्रियास्तथा ॥"

Sāmba Purana, 16-87 to 88 (or, in some
editions, 26-30 to 31) :—

"मगाश्च मामगाश्चैव मानसा मन्दगास्तथा ।
मगा ब्राह्मणभूयिष्ठा मामगाः क्षत्रियास्तथा ॥"

Padma Purana, Swarga Khanda, 8-34 :—

"मगाश्च मप्रकाश्चैव मानसा मल्लकास्तथा ।
मगाश्च ब्रह्मभूयिष्ठाः खकर्मनिरता द्विजाः ॥"

(138)

[In some editions the reading is म्रगाश्च
for मगाश्च। See the St. Petersburg Dictionary, under म्रग।]

Page 45. (Conclusion).

Note 1.   Suta Samhita, 4-20-16 :—

"समूलेषु च धर्म्मेषु बुद्धागमसमन्वितः।
धर्म्मः श्रेष्ठ इति प्रोक्तो मया वेदार्थपारगाः॥"

Page 46.

Note. 1.   In Huc's Travels it is said that Ksong-ka-pa
derived his tenents partly from Buddhism
but chiefly from Christianity, through a
Roman Catholic Missionary with whom
he came in contact. Similar evidences
are gathered by Prinsep in his " Tibet,
Tartary and Mongolia."

A parallel among the Christian Fathers
to the Buddhist sect of Apagata-pada-
mrakshana or those who were " never
guilty of washing their feet " is to be
found in St. Anthony, the patriarch of
monachism. [See Maudsley : Body and
Mind, Psychological Essays, p. 117.]

Page 47.

Note 1.   Introduction to the Astasāhasrikā :—

भगवती-प्रज्ञापारमिता-स्तोत्रम्।
" ॐ नमो भगवत्यै आर्य्यप्रज्ञापारमितायै।

निर्विकल्पे नमस्तुभ्यं प्रज्ञापारमितेऽमिते ।

या त्वं सर्वानवद्याङ्गि निरवद्यैर्निरीच्यसे ॥ ”

Note 2.   Agni Purana, 49-8 :—

“ प्रान्तात्मा लम्बकर्णश्च गौराङ्गश्वाम्बराष्टतः ।

ऊर्द्धपद्मास्थितो बुद्धो वरदाभयदायकः ॥ ”

Page 48.

Note 1.   Rig Veda, Khila Sukta, 28-6 : —

“ अग्निं प्रत्यच्चदैवतम् । ”

Brihannāradiya Purana, 2-39 :—

“ भूभ्रादिलोकैश्चितयं संहृत्यात्मानमात्मना ।

पश्यन्ति योगिनः सर्वे तमीशानं भजाम्यहम् ॥ ”

(The context would show that the verse refers to Buddha).

Page 49.

Note 2.   Cunningham : Coins   of   Ancient   India, pp. 75-78 :—

“ The Yaudheyas were one of the most famous tribes of Ancient India.

“ The coins of the Yaudheyas * * are of two distinct kinds ; the older ones dating from about the first century B.C., and the later ones dating from about A.D. 300.

“ A third class are, perhaps, of a slightly later date.   They are remarkable for having a six-headed figure on one side.

This figure ought to be Kartikeya, who is named " six-headed." These later coins must, therefore, be Brahminical.

" Plate VI. Fig. 1. The type is a Bodhi tree with Buddhist railing, and four small circles.

" Plate VI. Figs. 2, 3. Obverse: Indian Legend, Yaudheyani. Reverse: Combine symbol of Tri-ratna and Dharma-chakra.

" Plate VI. Fig. 9. Obverse: Six-headed male figure. Indian Legend, Bhāgavato Swamina Brāhmana Yaudheya. Reverse : Six-headed figure standing to front between Chaitya and Bodhi tree."

Page 50.

Note 1.   Vachaspati Misra : Nyāyavārtika-Tātparya-tikā, p. 300 (in the Vizianagram Series):

" नहि प्रमाणीकृतबौद्धाद्यागमा अपि लोकयात्रायां श्रुतिस्मृतीतिहासपुराणनिरपेच्छागममात्रेण प्रवर्त्तन्ते । अपि तु तेऽपि सांवृतमेतदिति ब्रुवाणा लोकयात्रायां श्रुत्यादीने वानुसरन्ति ।"

English Translation :—

The Buddhist āgamas, of which the authority is vainly supported, depend for all that concerns the practical life upon the Sruti, the Smriti, the Itihāsas, the

Purānas. Buddhists themselves do not fear to say: 'It is the custom (sāmvrtam etat),' and they follow, in practical life, Revelation and Tradition.

[Quoted from Vallee Poussin's "Authority of Buddhist Agamas" in p. 376 of the Journal of the Royal Asiatic Society, 1902.]

Page 53.

Note 2. Sankarachārya in his Dasāvatāra Stotram :—

"य आस्ते कलौ योगिनां चक्रवर्त्तौ
स बुद्धः प्रबुद्धोऽस्तु मच्चित्तवर्तौ ।"

Page 54.

Note 1. Taranath is the same as Kun-snjing of Thibet.

Note 2. Padma Purana, Kriyā Khanda, 6-188 :—

"वेदाः विनिन्दिता येन विलोक्य पशुहिंसनम् ।
सङ्क्षेपेन त्वया येन तस्मै बुद्धाय ते नमः ॥"

Bhagavata Purana, 11-4-22 :—

"वादैर्विमोहयति यज्ञकृतोऽतदर्हान् ।"

Sankara Vijaya, 12-8 :—

"प्रायः क्रतुद्वेषकृतादराय बोधैकधाम्ने स्पृहयामि भूम्ने ।"

Gita Govindam, Hymn to the Avatāras :—

"निन्दसि यज्ञविधेरह्ह श्रुतिजातम् ।
सदयहृदयदर्शितपशुघातम् ।
केशवधृतबुद्धशरीर जय जगदीश हरे ।"

Page 55.

Note 1. Mundaka Upanishad, 1-2-7 to 10 :—

"प्लवा ह्येते अदृढा यज्ञरूपा

* * लोकं ह्रीनतरं चाविश्रन्ति ॥"

Gough : Philosophy of the Upanishads, p. 102. (Translation of the above) :—

"Sacrifices with their ritual and its eighteen parts are frail boats indeed ; and they that rejoice in sacrifice as the best of things, in their infatuation shall pass on again to decay and death" (i.e., shall be again born in the mortal sphere).

Purport :—The ceremonial rites which are attended with animal sacrifices can not lift a man above the mortal sphere at his death. Those who perform works which confer benefits on others, if they think that to be the highest duty of man, go to heaven, but subsequently return again to the mortal sphere. (Means to say that the acquisition of gnosis must be joined to the performance of good works in order to give man a permanent place among the immortals. *Cf.* Isavasya Upanishad, verses 9-11.)

Bhagavadgita, 2-42 to 46 :—

"यामिमां पुष्पितां वाचं प्रवदंत्यविपश्चितः ।

(143)

*　　*　　*

क्रियाविशेषबहुलां भोगैश्वर्य्यगतिं प्रति ॥

*　　*　　*

त्रैगुण्यविषया वेदा निस्त्रैगुण्यो भवार्जुन । ''

etc., etc.

Purport :—The elaborate rites and cere-monials which have accreted round Vedic worship had better be dispensed with.

Page 56.

Note 1.　Padma Purana, quoted by Vijnāna Bhik-shu :—

"दैत्यानां नाशनार्थाय विष्णुना बुद्धरूपिणा ।

बौद्धशास्त्रमसत्प्रोक्तं नग्ननीलपटादिकम् ॥

वेदार्थवन्महाशास्त्रं मायावादमवैदिकम् ।

मयैव कथितं देवि जगतां नाशकारणात् ॥

मायावादमसच्छास्त्रं प्रच्छन्नं बौद्धमेव तत् ।

मयैव कथितं देवि कलौ ब्राह्मणरूपिणा ॥ ''

—Sankhya Pravachana Bhashya, 1-22.

(See also Garbe's Edition, Harvard, p. 16, lines 7–11.)

Page 59.

Note 2.　Chhandogya Upanishad, 5-10-7 :—

"तद्य इह रमणीयचरणा अभ्याशो ह यत्ते रमणीयां योनिमापद्येरन् । ''

Max Muller, Lectures, quoted in Shome's "Old Gaya and Gayawals."　(P. 38.)

Page 63.

Note 2. Brihadaranyaka Upanishad, 4-4-13, (also Satapatha Brahmana, 14-7-2-17) :—

" यस्यानुवित्तः प्रतिबुद्ध आत्माऽस्मिन् देहे गहने प्रविष्टः ।
स विश्वकृत् स हि सर्वस्य कर्त्ता तस्य लोकः स उ लोक एव ॥ "

Page 66.

Note 3. " Nirvana is the only thing which does not arise as the effect of a cause, and which as cause again does not give rise to any effect."—Dahlke : Buddhist Essays (Silācāra's Translation, p. 88).

Page 67.

Note 1. Mahaparinirvana Sutra, Ch. 5, § 6 :—

Culture of the Will and Duty in Buddhism (Mahaparinirvana Sutra, Ch. 2, § 33 ; Ch. 5, §§ 4–6) :—

" Therefore, O Ananda, be ye lamps unto yourselves. Be ye a refuge to yourselves. Betake yourselves to no external refuge. Hold fast to the truth as a lamp. Hold as a refuge to the truth. Look not for refuge to anyone beside yourselves."

" Now at that time the twin Sāla trees were all one mass of bloom with flowers out of season ; and all over the body of the Tathāgata these dropped and

[P. 67 (cont.)]

sprinkled and scattered themselves, out of reverence for the successor of the Buddhas of old..... And heavenly sandalwood powder and Mandaru flowers, ... and heavenly music, ... and heavenly songs came wafted from the skies, out of reverence for the successor of the Buddhas of old! Then the Blessed One addressed the venerable Ananda, and said : 'Now it is not thus, Ananda, that the Tathāgata is rightly honoured, reverenced, venerated, held sacred or revered. But the brother or the sister, the devout man or the devout woman, who continually fulfils all the greater and the lesser duties, who is correct in life, walking according to the precepts—it is he who rightly honours, reverences, venerates, holds sacred and reveres the Tathāgata with the worthiest homage. Therefore, O Ananda, be ye constant in the fulfilment of the greater and the lesser duties, and be ye correct in life, walking according to the precepts ; and thus, Ananda, should it be taught.'"

Note 2.	The Rig Veda Samhita, beginning : "अग्निमीळे पुरोहितम् ।"

[P. 67 (cont.)]

The Black Yajur Veda, 1-5-10-2 ; the Katha Samhita (Charaka Sākhā), 7-14 ; the Samavidhāna Brahmana, 3-4-4 :—

"अयमग्निः श्रेष्ठतमः ।"

Taittiriya Brahmana, 2-4-3-3 :—

"अग्निरग्रे प्रथमो देवानाम् ।"

Mahabharata, Rājadharma, 8-37 :—

"प्राग्स्वतोऽयं भूतिपथो नास्त्यन्तमनुशुश्रुम ।"

Commentary :—[अनादिरनन्तत्वायं यज्ञियः पन्था इत्यर्थः । नीलकांठः ।]

The same, 60-52 :—

"स्तेनो वा यदि वा पापो यदि वा पापकृत्तमः ।
यष्टुमिच्छति यज्ञं यः साधुमेव वदन्ति तम् ॥"

(This seems to have been the original meaning of the terms Sādhu and Sādhanā. Sadhu is one who performs (in Sanskrit, Sādhaté) the Yajna. Yajna is the rite of the Sacred Fire. Its association with sacrifice is a subsequent affair

Sankarāchārya : Sādhanapanchaka, verse 1 :—

"वेदो नित्यमधीयतां तदुदितं कर्म्म खनुष्ठीयताम् ।"

Purport :—Study the one principal Veda (the Rig-Veda) and do the one work it prescribes. This one work, as is known to all students of the Rig-Veda, is Agnihotra, or worship of the Sacred Fire. See Sankarāchārya's own gloss on the word

"Karma" in Isopanishad-bhāsya (Mantras 2 and 11).

Page 70.   (Appendix.)

Note 2.   Mahabharata, Rājadharma, 15-49 :—

"अहिंसा साधुहिंसा ।"

Purport :—Sparing the wicked is killing the righteous. The real meaning of the term 'Ahinsā' comes out in this text. It cannot mean animal-sacrifice. It means "total absence of hatred towards wrong," i.e., absolute forgiveness of injuries.

Page 71.

Note 1.   Vidyaranya's Jivanmukti-viveka, Ch. 2 :—

"नमोऽस्तु कोपदेवाय क्षात्रयज्वालिने भ्रग्नम् ।"

Page 73.

Note 1.   Mahabharata, Udyogaparva, 33-48 ff. :—

"एकः क्षमावतां दोषो द्वितीयो नोपपद्यते ।
यदेनं क्षमया युक्तमशक्तं मन्यते जनः ॥
सोऽस्य दोषो न मन्तव्यः क्षमा हि परमं बलम् ।
क्षमा गुणो ह्यशक्तानां शक्तानां भूषणं क्षमा ॥"

The same, Dronaparva, 198-59 :—

"वयं क्षमयितारश्च किमन्यत्र प्रमाद्यत ।"

Purport :—The all-forgiving man is thought to be weak and worthless. Still, forgiveness is the highest virtue, as it ensures peace, than which nothing can be higher.

Pascal : The quotation is from Adams in his Secret of Success, p. 222.

Note 3.   Rig Veda, 6-48-10 ; Sama Veda, 2-974 :—

"हेडांसि दैव्या युयोधि नोऽदेवानि व्हरांसि च ।"

Purport :—Remove all natural despites and ungodlike abhorrences.

Isāvāsya Upanishad, 6 :—

"ततो न विजुगुप्सते ।"

Purport :—A man would naturally cease to hate (when he beholds that the Self which is his is the Self in all living beings).

Page 74.

Note 1.   Dhammapada, 26-17, Pali Text :—

"अक्कोसं बधबन्धं च अदुट्ठो यो तितिक्खति ।
खन्तीबलं बलानिकं तमहं ब्रूमि ब्राह्मणं ॥"

[Sans.—अक्रोशन् बधबन्धौ च अदुष्टो यस्तितिच्छति ।
क्षान्तिबलं बलानीकं तमहं ब्रवीमि ब्राह्मणम् ॥]

—This saying is justly held to be unparalleled.

Page 76.

Note 1.   The entire passage has been quoted from memory, the original source having been forgotten.

POSTSCRIPT.—Bearing in mind that in slaughter lies the germ of hatred (cf. the beginning of the Appendix), it may be easily understood that Religion, which seeks to promote love can never give countenance to the slaughter of any living creature, although that regrettable custom might arise through necessity. But custom is not religion in every case.

The Appendix is a literary essay and does not properly fit in with the main book. It has been retained to show the true meaning of Ahinsa, which is the cardinal doctrine of Buddhism and about which there has been much misunderstanding. For, too often it is supposed that Buddha's whole religion consisted in preventing the slaughter of animals and that Ahinsā in Buddhism means nothing more than desisting from such slaughter. But this cannot be the truth. He who thoroughly comprehended the law of Nature which ordains that animals should prey upon one another for their food and sustenance, and who made this law the basis of his doctine of Karma (or Retribution) and of the moral system arising out of that doctrine, could never have been so sensitive to animal sacrifices as he is supposed to have been. This supposition arose from Buddha's opposition to making animal sacrifice a part of religion, as was done in his time by the Brahmanas when performing the rites of the Yajna or Sacred Fire. The Brahmanas themselves, however, were systematically opposed to animal slaughter except when it was done as part of some Yajna or religious rite; for they considered that in such cases the soul of the victim

20

ascends to heaven, and that in return for this act of mercy and benevolence, it takes to heaven the soul of the sacrificer afterwards at the time of his death. Therefore do the Brahmanas say that animal sacrifice in Yajna is not an act of *Hinsā* (*or antipathy*) but an act of *Ahinsā* (*or sympathy*); but they hold that elsewhere than in Yajna animal slaughter is always an act of Hinsā or antipathy. (In connection with this Brahmanical creed, see Rev. Dr. K. M. Banerji's Tract on the Relation between Christianity and Hinduism, and Dr. Law's Article on the Education of the Jainas.) The term "Ahinsā" occurs in the Upanishads; and comparing the Chhāndōgya Upanishad (3-17-4) with the Brihadāranyaka Upanishad (5-2-3), it would be found that the original meaning of the term is the same as "*Dayā*," which is synonymous with sympathy, love, mercy, benevolence, etc. That this is the real meaning of the term is determined by the text of the Mahabharata quoted above (p. 147, line 7), which says that "Ahinsā towards the wicked is Hinsā towards the virtuous." In this text, Ahinsā cannot be taken to mean sacrifice of animals; the term evidently means 'total absence of hatred towards wrong,' *i.e.*, absolute forgiveness of all injuries;—and the whole text, which literally means "sparing the wicked is killing the righteous," aims to give expression to the fact that charity is the negation of morality.

INDEX.

INDEX.

(Esp. to subjects which occur in more than one place.)

[The number refers to pages, and (n) refers to foot-notes.]

A

Æsop's Fables—their origin in the Jataka-tales of Buddhism, 20(n).

Ahinsa—its Hinduistic origin, 19(n), 73; its real import, 69ff., 147, 149.

Amara Singha—a Hindu follower of Buddha, 31, 49(n).

Angels—[See Bible and Gods].

Anti-Vedic—Buddhism wrongly supposed to be, 54; Doctrine of Ahinsa wrongly supposed to be, 73; Doctrine of Maya held to be, 55–56.

Arabian Nights (The)—their origin from Indian sources, 20(n).

Asceticism—Buddha representative of, 27, 28(n); Buddhism a reformation of, 13, 50, 51; Buddhists a sect of, 55(n).

Asoka—The time of, 32(n), 63.

Atheism—Buddha saves the Vedas from the influence of, 38–40, 135, 136; Buddha's attitude towards, 37, 64; Buddhism not, 21(n), 58; leads to theism, 37, 130.

Avatara—Buddha an, 25, 35–37, 109; Function of, 26(n), 36, 39, 109, 134; Place of Buddha in the line of, 66.

Avesta—Elements of the Upanishads in the, 78.

B

Barābudur—Barābhayada posture in the images of, 48(n); Tilaka and Yajnōpavita in the images of, 28(n). [See also Java.]

Bible— compared with Rig-Veda, 87ff; confirms rightful hatred, 72(n); inculcates love to enemy, 73(n); Angels in the, 3(n), 4, 79; The cow in the, 6(n), 87; The Sacred Fire in the, 4, 81ff, 85; on the spirit, 78. [See Christianity.]

Hindu follower of Buddha, 49 ; a later day erection, 31(n) ; Old Indian name of, 43(n) ; Story of the image in, 89.

Buddhism—a reformation of Hinduism, 7, 50, 57(n. 1), 59, 60, 63, 64 ; Sectarianism in 33, 41(n), 45ff, 52, 53, 53(n), 55(n), 58, 58(n. 2), 64(n), 115, 138 ; Foreigners in, 42, 45(n), 52, 54, 58(n), 74(n. 3) ; 122 ; God in, 21, 58, 60, 62, 65 ; Hindu symbols in, 28(n), 47(n), 48, 116, 127 ; Āgamas of, 115, 138, 140 ; The cardinal doctrine of, 149 ; Persecution of, 52, 58(n) ; Royal patronage to, 42(n), 49 ; Temples of, 10, 34, 43(n) ; its relation to Tantra, 11, 45–47 ; its inadequacy explained, 50.

Buddhists—their personal laws and customs originally same as those of Hindus, 49–51.

Burma—mentioned, 42, 43(n), 45(n).

Burning the dead—in Hinduism, 6 ; in Buddhism, 14.

Butter—in Hinduism, 5 ; in Buddhism, 10 ; in Christianity, 87 in Mysticism, 88.

C

Castes—Buddha takes food from all, 13, 15 ; differ in the method of their Buddha-adoration, 122 ; Buddha admits higher and lower in, 12, 64.

Chaitya—Meaning of, 49 (n. 2) ; Origin of, 10, 92 ; symbolised in Hindu coins, 49, 140.

Charity—as negation of morality, 70 ; as higher than the intellect, 73 (n. 1).

Christianity—Buddhism and, 46 (n), 138 ; Persecution and, 58 (n).

Cow—her universal worship prophesied in the Bible, 6 (n), 87 ; worshipped by Hindus, 5, 86 ; worshipped by Buddhists, 10.

D

Desirelessness—a Hinduistic doctrine, 24, 65 ; Buddha teaches the doctrine of, 24, 51 (n), 65, 66 (n), 99 ff.

Devas—[See Gods].

Devadatta—his enmity to Buddha, 16, 41.

Dharma—a Hinduistic term, 63 ; a name for the Religion of Buddhism, 32, 52 (n), 60 ; its practice incomplete without the study of the Vedas, 60 (n). [See also Sanatana Dharma.]

Dharmapala—the Anāgārika Bauddhāchārya, 50 (n), 52 (n), 58 (n) ; a name of Buddha, 32.

Dharmaraja—a name of Buddha, 32, 52 (n), 127.

Dharmeshwara—a name of Buddha, 32, 126.

Dharma-Thakur—a name of Buddha, 33, 52 (n), 122.

Dream—Buddha accepts the Vedantic philosophy of life as a, 22, 102.

Druj—the Avestic term for the Vedic Māyā, 2 (n), 79.

Duty—The Vedic doctrine of, 4 ; Buddha teaches the Vedic doctrine of, 24, 67, 145.

F

False doctrine—of Nihilism, 22, 40 ; of Māyā, 56.

Fire (The Sacred)—in the Bible, 4, 81, 82, 85 ; in Buddhism, 9, 9 (n.3), 11, 121 ; in Chinese and Parsi Religions, 3 (n) ; in the Tantras, 11 ; in the Vedas, 4, 48, 80, 83–86, 88, 146 ; and the sun, 9 ; and the Lingam-Yoni, 5 (n), 84, 86 ; produced by friction, 5 (n.1), 30 (n) ; its mysterious power of revelation, 5 (n.1), 48, 81, 82, 84, 86, 88 ; the rationale of its power, 4, 83.

Free-will—Buddhism ignores the doctrine of the, 50 ; To forgive and forget is the highest achievement of the, 75.

G

Ghrita—[See Butter].

Gita (or the Bhagavad-Gita)—and Buddhism, 24, 55 ; referred to, 26 (n), 39, 72 (n).

Gods (angels, devas, fairies, spirits)—and goddesses, 47 (n), 84 ; and idolatry, 48 (n), 114 ; in the Bible, 79 ; in the Koran, 79 ff ; in Buddhism, 11, 59, 92, 96, 124 ; in the Vedas, 3 ; in the Tantras, 11 ; are beings with bodies of fire, 4, 83 ; Classes of, 79, 92 ff., 124 ; their morals, 72 ; their appearance to man, 48 (n) ; Methods of invoking the, 4, 23 (n.3), 48 (n), 84, 85, 104.

H

Hallucinations—and Yoga, 23, 48.

Haraprasad Sastri (President, Asiatic Society)—Facts on Bud dhism brought to light by, 33 (n), 52 (n). [*No scholar has done so much to clear up obscure and unknown points in Bud-dhism.*]

Hatred—The Vedas anticipate Buddha's teachings concerning, 19 19 (n) ; 73 ; 147 ff ; ceases by love, 19, 72 ; its germ in slaugh ter, 148 ; its necessity, 69. 72 (n). [*N.B.* The Sanskrit word bharansi (p. 147) suggests the English word abhorrence, with which it has the same meaning.]

Householders—Original Buddhism not for, 50 ; Modified Bud-dhism for, 60 (n).

I

Idols (or images)—Distinguishing feature of Buddhistic, 116, 127 ; Distinguishing feature of Jaina, 33 (n) ; Hinduistic origin of, 11 (n), 26, 28 (n), 45, 47, 48 (n) ; Meaning of temples having obscene, 95 ; Story of Buddha's original, 89 ; Buddha's sym-bolical, (Buddhapada and Salagrama), 57. 114 ff.

Ignoring—of the Vedas, 59 ; of God, 60 ; of the super-sensual. 61.

Immortality—[See Soul].

Incarnation—[See Avatāra].

J

Jagatjit Singh, Maharaja of Kapurthala,—referred to, 45 (n).

Jātaka-tales (of Buddhism)—the original of Æsop's Fables, 20 (n) ; The theme of the, 20 (n) ; Mahabharata and the, 17 (n) ; Buddhist story of King Rama in the, 66 (n) ; Vedas accepted for Buddhists by the, 60 (n).

Jātaka-sasthi Puja—Hindus invoke Buddha in the, 120.

Java—Monuments of Indian character in, 45 (n), 116. [See Barabudur.]

Jesus—a typical Yogin, 105.

(158)

K

Kali Age—Buddha the highest personality of the, 108, 136; referred to, 56.

Kapila—Relation of Buddha to, 112.

Kapila-vāstu (or abode of Kapila)—the birth-place of Buddha, 7, 37, 40, 41, 112.

Karma—Belief in the survival of the soul is involved in the doctrine of, 59: a Hinduistic doctrine, 19: True Buddhism higher than the doctrine of, 74; The doctrine of Niskāma, 24.

Kikatas—name of modern Bihar, 42; play-ground of Buddha's activities, 34, 37, 41; Significance of the plural number in, 36—37; 37 (n).

Knowledge and Work—Evolution is the result of a combination of, 105 ff, 142.

Koran (The)—Angels in, 3 (n), 79; supports rightful hatred, 72 (n).

Krishna—referred to, 20 (n), 39, 41, 46.

L

Lingam (The)— in its origin not Phallic but Vedic, being a symbol for the Sacred Fire, 6 (n), 10 (n.3), 86. [See Yoni.]

Love (Universal)—same as Ahinsa, 73, 150; a Vedic doctrine, 19; begins with love to enemy, 72.

M

Magadha—Disquisition on the word, 42; equivalent to Kikata, 37 (n).

Mahabharata—Ahinsa in, 19 (n.1), 94; Buddha in, 26 (n), 110.

Mandana Misra—Sankarāchārya was opposed not to Buddha but to, 52 (n), 55 (n).

Mantram (or incantation)—in Buddhism, 29, 45, 46, 121.

Marriage—Hindu doctrine of the sanctity of, 6; Buddha upholds the doctrine of the sanctity of 19, 51.

Maya —a Vedic doctrine, 21, 99, 132 ; akin to Nihilism, 22, 38,
55ff, 132 ; its likeness to dream, 22, 99 ;—stone of Mexico,
74 (n) ; same as the Will or creative power in Nature, 2, 79,
99.

Meditation—Depth of Buddha's, 20, 23 (n.3), 98, 124 ; on Buddha,
28, 118 ; Yoga-powers inherent in, 23 (n), 48 (n).

Metaphysics (of Buddha)—based on the Vedas, 20ff ; anticipates
the modern doctrine of Will, 66 (n).

Muhammadans—acquainted with Buddha, 15, 48(n), 74 (n) ; as
persecutors, 58 (n). [See also Koran.]

Mysteries of the Hindu Religion—viz.,—communion with gods,
48, 84 ; seeing the Self, 23, 104 ; attainment of Nirvāna or
perpetual peace (the life eternal), 3, 88, 99-103.

N

Nahar Museum—referred to, 128.

Narayana—Hindus hold Buddha to be an incarnation of, 25, 108,
109 ; Buddhists admit Buddha to be, 26.

Nepal— the native land of Buddha, 7 ; a land of meat-eaters,
8 (n) ; Buddha worshipped by the Hindus of, 53 (n).

Nihilism—[See Sunyatā].

Nirvana—a Hinduistic doctrine, 3, 22 (n), 63 ; Attainment of,
(through extinction of desires), 99ff, (or through practice of
devotion), 121 ; Meaning of, 59 (n), 66 (n.3) ; the uncaused
cause and the action without a reaction, 66 (n), 144.

O

" Om mani padme hum "—the Buddhist Mantram (in its origin
Tantrika), 46 ; formulated by Padmapani, 54 (n) ; References
for the exposition of, 47 (n).

P

Panis—referred to, 86.

Persecution—True Buddhism never suffered, 52 (n.3), 57, 63 ;
Corrupt Buddhism subjected by Shashanka to, 52, 58 (n) ;
Effect on Buddhism of Muhammadan, 58 (n).

T

PLATES.

THE BARĀBHAYA.
Buddha offering protection.*

From the Indian Museum (Br. 9.—Bihar).

Photo by A. B. Maitreya of the Indian Museum (Calcutta)

(For explanation see p. 169.)

* More properly, offering boon and protection. The boon is supposed to be in the hand which is lying on the lap. It may be more or less raised up or it may be kept as it is in the plate.

EXPLANATION OF PLATE I.

This plate shows both the Tilaka-mark on the forehead and the Barābhayada posture of the hands in the images of Buddha. It is to face page 27 and page 28 (n. 1), and also to face page 47 and page 48 (n. 1). Both the Tilaka-mark and the Barābhayada posture are symbols in Hindu mysticism, and their presence in Buddha's images proves the latter to have been objects of Hindu worship. The injunction to the worshipper to wear the Tilaka himself on his forehead carries with it the injunction to put the same on the forehead of the idol of his worship. Buddha used to wear the Tilaka himself, for the Tilaka is represented on the forehead of the image of the goddess whom he worshipped (Prajnāpāramitā, or Tārā, or Kuan-yin). The Tilaka was continued to be worn by Buddha's successors and is visible in the images of Avalokiteshwara and others. A kind of Tilaka in the shape of three parallel horizontal lines on the forehead, called by the Hindus the Tripundra and much worn by them, is to be found depicted on the forehead of the images of such prominent Buddhist Missionaries as Bodhidharma, Asanga, etc. (see p. 47, note 1). The Tilaka for the Hindu worshippers of Buddha has been ordained to resemble the leaf of the Aswattha tree (the *ficus religiosa*), and is to be painted with the paste of yellow sandal wood as directed by the Suta Samhita in the Text quoted below.

The Barābhayada posture of a deity is a peculiarly Hindu conception. It can have no place in any atheistic or nihilistic system of thought, for it involves the ideas of the existence of an Almighty and Benevolent Deity, of a host of Angels, of Paradise and the life to come, of the soul and its immortality. Its meaning is that man can commune in spirit with the mysterious power of Nature, and receive therefrom the object of his desires and a protection from all fears. No Hindu's worship is complete without meditation on his Deity in this posture.

A comparison of Buddhistic images having the Tilaka and the Barābhayada-Mudra with Hinduistic images of the same description, would undoubtedly tend to prove that they all had their origin from a common source.

REFERENCES.

The above photograph is from an image in the Indian Museum, Magadha Section (800-1200 A.D.), Br. 9, Bihar. It shows, as has been said above, both the Tilaka and the Barābhayada posture in one.

The Tilaka-mark on Buddha :—Statues of this description may be seen at the Barabudur, Java; at the Boston Museum, U.S.A.; at the Buddha-Gaya Temple, India; at Dharmapāla's Collection, Nahar's Collection, and the Indian Museum, Calcutta; at the Louvre, Paris; at the Imperial Museums of Tokyo and Kyoto, and at Kamakura, Japan.

For photographs of Tibetan and Burmese images of Buddha having the Tilaka on the forehead, see H. G. Wells: Short History of the World, pages 151 and 152; for Ceylonese images of the same description, see Woodward: Pictures of Buddhist Ceylon, frontispiece; for Chinese images of the same description, see Ashton: Study of Chinese Sculpture, the Plates,—especially plate 53 (Buddha in Maitreya's Paradise); for Javan images of the same description, see Karl With: Java, plates 10, 11, 12, 29, 33; for Japanese images of the same description, see M. Anesaki: Buddhist Art, plates 11, 12, 14; for Central Asian images of the same description, see Foucher: Beginnings of Buddhist Art, plates 11, 13.

The Tilaka-mark on Buddha's Deity (Prajnāpāramitā, or Tārā or Kuan-yin) :—Statues of this description may be seen at the Leiden Museum, Holland; at the Eumorfopoulos and the Raphael Collections, London.

For photographs of the above, see Karl With : Java, plate 102; Ashton : Study of Chinese Sculpture, frontispiece and plate 57.

The Tilaka-mark on Buddha's successors (Avalokiteshwara, Manjusri, etc.) :—Statues of this description may be seen at the Havemeyer Collection, New York, and the Freer Collection, Washington, U.S.A.; at the Louvre, Paris; at the Barabudur, Java.

For photographs of the above, see Ashton : Study of Chinese Sculpture, plates 25, 27, 30; Karl With : Java, plate 59. [For

Tilaka on the Twenty-five Bodhisattwas, see Anesaki : Buddhist Art, plate 11.]

The Tilaka-mark (called Tripundra) on Buddhist Missionaries (Asanga etc.) :—Statues of this description are abundant in Nepal, Tibet, China, Japan, Mongolia and Siberia. Photos of the same may be seen in books of Travels or of Art, relating to those countries, although most of the images have not been identified by the Authors. A small image of Asanga may be seen at the Reception-House of Rai Biharilala Mitra Bahadur, Zamindar, Calcutta ; and a picture of the same may be seen in the Toyo Bijutsu Shu, or Pictures of Oriental Arts : Part 2, plate 1. (Kokkasha, Tokio, Japan.)

The Barābhayada posture of Buddha :—Statues of this description may be seen at the Museum of Fine Arts, Boston, U.S.A. ; at the Barābudur, Java ; at the Indian Museum, Calcutta, and at the Temple, Buddha-Gaya, India. (For Bara-Abhaya Mudras in Javan images, see Foucher : Beginnings of Buddhist Art, p. 256.)

For photographs of the above, see Karl With : Java, plates 9, 11, 12, 33, 95 ; Ashton : Study of Chinese Sculpture, plate 42 (a). Most of Buddha's photos taken by tourists in India are of this description. The Hindu pictures of Dasāvatāra always show Buddha in this Barābhayada posture.

The Tilaka-mark on the forehead of, and the Barābhayada-mudra in the hands of, a Hindu Deity :—Statues of this description may be seen in Hindu Temples all over India. And photographs or pictures of the same are kept by all Hindus in their houses.

Up to the present times all orthodox Hindus have continued to put the Tilaka-mark on their own forehead as well as on the forehead of their idols ; and when they meditate on their Deity, they invest it with the Barābhayada posture.

ORIGINAL TEXTS.

For the Tilaka-mark :—

(*a*) of Buddha-worship in particular :

अश्वत्थपत्रसदृशां हरिचन्दनेन

मध्ये ललाटमतिशोभनमादरेण ।

बुद्धागमे मुनिवरा यदि संस्कृतस्ये-
न्मुद्राक्षिणा सततमेव तु धारयेच ॥

—Suta Samhita, Suta Gita, 8-34.

(*b*) of Hindu-worship in general :

काम्यं नैमित्तिकं नित्यं यत्किञ्चित्कर्म्म नारद ।

वर्णाश्रमाणां तन्नास्ति स्नानान्ते तिलकं विना ॥

—Padma Purana, Uttarakhanda.

For the Barābhayada posture :—

(*a*) of Buddha in particular :

श्रान्तात्मा लम्बकर्णश्च गौराङ्गश्वाम्बराहतः ।

ऊर्द्धपद्मास्थितो बुद्धो वरदाभयदायकः ॥

—Agni Purana, 49-8.

(*b*) of Hindu Deities in general :—

वरदाभयशूलविषाणधरं प्रणमामि शिवं शिवकल्पतरुम् ।

—Nityakarma, Sivastotra, 6. [Siva is the God of
Saivas, as Buddha is of Bauddhas.]

नित्यानन्दकरी वराभयकरी सौन्दर्यरत्नाकरी ।

निधुताखिलघोरपावनकरी प्रत्यच्चमहेश्वरी ॥

—Sankara's Annapurnā Devi stotra, 1. [The
Devi or Goddess is the same as Tārā or
Prajnāpāramitā of Buddha.]

प्रातः शिरसि शुक्लाब्जे द्विनेचं द्विभुजं गुरुम् ।

वराभयकरं श्रान्तं स्मरेत्तन्नामपूर्वकम् ॥

—Guru Gita, Guru-stotra, the Dhyana. [The
Guru is here identified with the Deity.]

THE YAJNŌPAVITA.
Buddha wearing the Sacred Thread.

From the Barabudur (upper and lower Balustrades).

Designed by Yogiraja's Disciple Maitreya (Buddha Gaya).

(For explanation see p. 175.)

N.B.—Both the breasts are shown to indicate that the line is the sacred thread. Where only the right breast is shown, the line indicates the border of a cloth that has been worn over the left shoulder.

EXPLANATION OF PLATE II.

This plate shows the Yajnōpavita or the Brahmanical sacred thread round the neck, which is shown in some of the images of Buddha. It is to face page 28 (n.1). The wearing of the sacred thread round the neck is a purely Hinduistic institution, monopolised by the higher castes to distinguish themselves from the lower castes. Buddha was a Kshatriya,—a higher caste, and must have therefore worn it, especially as he respected caste distinctions (See p. 12). It seems therefore that Buddha himself did not secede from Hinduism at any time, not even after preaching his reformation.

The objection is sometimes raised that no ceremony of Upanayana (or investiture with the sacred thread) of Buddha is mentioned in any of the biographical accounts of Buddha, e.g., the Lalita Vistara, etc. To this it may be pointed out in reply that neither in the Rāmāyana nor in the Mahābhārata is there any mention of the said ceremony for their heroes, although there cannot be any doubt of its having taken place. Readers of the Ramayana will remember that in those days persons born of the lower castes could, by dint of excellence in merit, lay claim to the sacred thread; and Hanumān, who is represented as half beast and half man, is admitted by all to have worn the sacred thread, which is visible in all the idols and pictures of that hero as worshipped by the Hindus. (See the verses of the Hanumat Kavacha in the Ānanda-Rāmāyana, quoted below.)

Doubts may be entertained, with more reasons, as to whether the dividing line, which is taken to be the sacred thread, may not really represent the border of the cloth worn by Buddha. For, indeed, an examination of the left hand in the images does show that a piece of cloth is thrown upon the left shoulder and wrapt round the breast in such a way as would make the border of the cloth run round the front in exactly the same way as would run the sacred thread. These doubts, however, are dispelled by some of the images showing two such dividing lines, one to represent

(176)

the border of the cloth, the other to indicate the sacred thread worn round the neck. Further, some of these images show one of the breasts as nude and exposed to view and the other as covered and hidden under the cloth ; while there are other images which show both the breasts nude, with the dividing line running between them. This may be taken to suggest that the dividing line in the latter class of images is meant to indicate the sacred thread while in the former class the same may be meant to indicate the border of the cloth. This might afford some support to the argument which just preceded.

A stronger evidence, however, is at hand ; namely, the evidence from the Jaina classical work, Tirthamālā-stavana. In this work there is a passage (quoted below) in which the Jaina Monk Saubhāgya Bijaya, who visited Buddha-Gaya about A.D. 1600, says that the images of Buddha are marked with the line of the Janoi (or Yajnopavita, the sacred thread) round the neck, and that such images are countless in number over there. He also adds that the Janoi-mark distinguishes Buddhist images from Jaina ones.

REFERENCES.

The above picture is a design made after the Barabudur images of Buddha.

Statues of this description may be seen at the Barabudur, Java ; at the Batavia Museum, Java ; at the Leiden Museum, Holland.

For photographs of the above, see Karl With : Java, plates 32, 33, 67, 95. For an image showing two dividing lines, one for the border of the cloth and the other for the sacred thread, see the same work, plate 32. For an image showing one breast as exposed and the other as covered by cloth, see the same work, plate 64.

ORIGINAL TEXTS.

For the Brahmanical sacred thread (or Yajnōpavita) worn by Buddha :—

तिच्यांथौ बोधगया कोस चक्ष छेरे ।

प्रतिमा बोधतख्यो नहिं पार रे ॥

जिनमुद्राथी विपरीत जाणजे रे ।

कराठ जनोइनो आकार रे ॥

> —Tirthamālā-stavana of Saubhāgya Bijaya,
> the Jaina Monk, who visited Buddha-Gaya
> about A.D. 1600 ; ch 10, verses 2 to 5.

For the sacred thread (or Yajnōpavita) worn by the Hindus :—

कार्पासन्तौमगोबालप्भररज्जुढणोद्भवम् ।

सदा सम्भवतो धार्य्यमुपवीतं द्विजातिभिः ॥

> —Devala-Smriti, on Yajnasutram.

The following texts prove that Hanumān, the hero of the Rāmāyana, wore the sacred thread :

"मौञ्जीयच्चोपवीताभरणरुचिग्निखं प्रोभितं कुण्डलाङ्कम् ।

--- हनुमन्तं विचिन्तयेत् ।" And again,

" दुकूलवसनं यच्चोपवीताजिनम् । - - - श्रीवायुपुत्रं भजेत् ।"

> —Ananda-Ramayana of Valmiki, in the
> Manohara Kanda, 13th Sarga. Also in Brah-
> manda Purana and in Sudarsana Samhita
> Tantra, in the Chapter on Hanumat Kavacham
> (twice in each).

MORE TITLES ON BUDDHISM
FROM PILGRIMS PUBLISHING

- A Buddhist Bible .... *Dwight Goddard*
- Basic Principles of Meditation .... *Richard Josephson*
- Buddha His Life, His Doctrine, His Order .... *Hermann Oldenberg*
- Buddhism, Its Essence and Development .... *Edward Conze*
- Buddhist Parables .... *Eugene Watson Burlingame*
- Buddhist Philosophy in India and Ceylon .... *A Berridale Keith*
- Buddhist Scriptures .... *E J Thomas*
- Esoteric Buddhism .... *A P Sinnett*
- Oracles and Demons of Tibet .... *Rene de Nebesky-Wojkowitz*
- Portrait of a Dalai Lama .... *Sir Charles Bell*
- Sacred Symbols of Buddhism .... *J R Santiago*
- Silent Meditation .... *H.E. Shamar Rinpoche*
- The Dharma-Samgraha .... *Edited by Kenjiu Kasawara*
- The Doctrine of Buddha .... *George Grimm*
- The Life of Milarepa .... *Translated by Lobsang P Lhalungpa*
- The Message of Buddha .... *A S wadia*
- The Milinda Questions .... *Mrs Rhys Davids*
- The Religion of Tibet .... *Sir Charles Bell*
- The Tibetan Book of the Dead .... *W Y Evans-Wentz, Lama Kazi Dawa-Sandup*
- The Tibetan Book of the Great Liberation .... *W Y Evans-Wentz*
- Thirty Pieces of Advice from the Heart .... *Gyalwa Longchenpa*
- Tibetan Religious Dances .... *Rene de Nebewsky-Wojkowitz*
- Tibetan Yoga and Secret Doctrines .... *Edited by W Y Evans-Wentz*
- Zen Buddhism .... *Christmas Humphreys*
- The Land of the Lamas .... *William Woodville Rockhill*
- Ngondro Commentary .... *Jane Tromge*
- Lord of the Dance .... *Chagdud Tulku*
- Delog .... *Delog Dawa Drolma*
- Gates to Buddhist Practice .... *Chagdud Tulku*
- P'howa Commentary .... *Chagdud Khadro*
- Red Tara Commentary .... *Chagdud Khadro*
- Life in Relation to Death .... *Chagdud Tulku*

www.pilgrimsbooks.com

For catalog and more information mail or fax to:

PILGRIMS BOOK HOUSE

Mail Order, P. O. Box 3872, Kathmandu, Nepal

Tel: 977-1-4700919 Fax: 977-1-4700943

E-mail: mailorder@pilgrims.wlink.com.np